Outside the Camp

The Wisdom, Humility, and Power of the Church

COLIN BROWN

WestBow
PRESS
A DIVISION OF THOMAS NELSON

Unless otherwise indicated, Scripture quotations are taken from *The Holy Bible, New International Version,* NIV® Copyright © 1973, 1978, 1984, 2011 by Biblica, Inc.,

Used by Permission. All rights reserved worldwide.

Scripture quotations marked "MSG" are taken from *The Message: The Bible in Contemporary Language.* Copyright © 2002 by Eugene H. Peterson. All rights reserved.

Scripture quotation marked "NLT" are taken from *The Holy Bible, New Living Translation,* copyright © 1996, 2004, 2007 by Tyndale House Foundation. Used by permission of Tyndale House Publishers Inc. All rights reserved.

WestBow Press books may be ordered through booksellers or by contacting:

WestBow Press
A Division of Thomas Nelson
1663 Liberty Drive
Bloomington, IN 47403
www.westbowpress.com
1 (866) 928-1240

ISBN: 978-1-4908-1000-3 (sc)
ISBN: 978-1-4908-1001-0 (hc)
ISBN: 978-1-4908-0999-1 (e)

Library of Congress Control Number: 2013917441

Printed in the United States of America.

WestBow Press rev. date: 9/26/2013

Table of Contents

Preface

Getting up from my chair and as good as staggering from it, I was almost overwhelmed by the good weight and sense of assurance with where I was heading with this book you are reading. I came to a halt on the floor in the passageway with another book open in hand. It was early afternoon on Friday, March 15, 2013.

During the previous hour, in a welcoming and frequented café setting, I had sat down for a totally unexpected God-appointed time with a good friend. The way it unfolded, lunch never happened!

I was with my cobber (that's "friend" or "mate" in the Australian vernacular), as I call Mark (who arrived with his wife, Bev, and their two boys from South Africa at the beginning of 2010).

During our conversation, Mark encouraged me in how he and our other brother and mate, Lynton, sensed the Lord's hand on the things I write. I went on to share with Mark for the first time about how I was well into having started writing this book. I had explained that of the number of books I had in progress in preparation for publishing, when I sought the Lord as to which one should I get published first, the Holy Spirit conveyed in no uncertain terms that *Outside the Camp* was it. I then shared with Mark some of what was in it.

On hearing where I was going with this book, Mark told me how only recently, Lynton had handed him the R. T. Kendall book *The Scandal of Christianity,* which I had never heard of. R. T.'s name alone was enough to make me sit up and take notice; I already owned other books of his. But when Mark told me the title of the last chapter of R. T.'s book, I was floored! Chapter 15 is "Outside the Camp."

Deep within, I was God-knowingly sure there was a connection and relationship between where I was going with my book and what Kendall had written. Not only was I stirred by just having heard that

R. T. had a chapter with the same title as this book, but I also knew I needed to read that chapter.

A short time following, I sat on my chair at home with R. T.'s book after Mark handed it over to me and after Lynton handed it to Mark. I intentionally only read that last chapter of R. T.'s book. It was as I began to read that I started to stagger from my chair.

As you read *Outside the Camp,* you will quite possibly begin to marvel with me at our God's resolve in re-landscaping and rebuilding his church his way, with the plumb line of his cornerstone.

"Not by might nor by power, but by my Spirit, says the LORD" (Zechariah 4:6).

Acknowledgments

Above all—far above all—I thank and praise the living, holy, and righteous One for his love, faithfulness, and extraordinary encouragement. Truly and assuredly, for the humble in heart and contrite in spirit, "He takes the clay, which is marred, and saves it from going to ruin and waste" (from a song I penned in 1994 and adapted from Jeremiah 18:1-11). What amazing grace; what a glorious Lord!

> Blessed be your glorious name, and may it be exalted above all blessing and praise. You alone are the LORD. You made the heavens, even the highest heavens, and all their starry host, the earth and all that is on it, the seas and all that is in them. You give life to everything, and the multitudes of heaven worship you. (Nehemiah 9:5-6)

God has made those for whom I mention here (and those whom I may fail to make worthy mention of) valuable, precious, and dear friends, brothers, and sisters (both natural and spiritual) and fellow soldiers.

To the most precious gift I have (after Jesus and my salvation) in my wonderful wife, Tina Maree—you are beautiful, altogether lovely, and amazing. How blessed can a man be? I love you deeply! Thank you with all my heart for your love, faithfulness, devotion, sacrifice, encouragement, and support of this, your man. The Lord bless you richly and eternally!

To our magnificent children (mentioned and not mentioned) and their blessed children (our grandchildren, to date), Sage and Dayna (Ziva); Hannah and Adrian (Andrew, Isabelle, and ?); Rebekkah "Bek"

(Amelia); Samuel; and our spiritual son, Michael (father of Andrew)—what a tribe, and what grace is this that you have filled our lives with such love, joy, learning, and even heartache. Bless you with the blessing of the Father from this father (and grandpa).

To Dad and Mum—blessed to be with our Lord Jesus and aware of just how truly great is God's grace in him. Thank you so much for loving me and instructing me.

To Lyn and John (for your loving and crucial support), Jenny (in your glorified home), and Mal (bro)—thank you for the love that you have all shown and the encouragement (naturally and prophetically) you have given me throughout my life. May the Lord bless you abundantly for it!

To "Sir" John, Rob, Rex, Fran, "Princess" Pat, Trish, Lynton and Amanda, Jenny, Leicester and Pauline, Chris and Heather, Ray and Anne, Dave, David, Peter and Colleen, and Mark and Bev for your real (genuine) friendship, fellowship, prayer, and service in walking in love with us through thick and thin—what a blessing you have been and are! Our God bless you, strengthen you, and encourage you in his great faithfulness.

To Rick, for pointing me higher—I salute you! Heaven on earth to you until you get to heaven once and for all. Thank you so much! Blessing to the *nth* degree in Jesus.

To "Deere Jack" for unknowingly reassuring and strengthening me.

To David and Narelle for your love, example, time, and support—much grace and blessing in the gracious One!

To Peter and Kaye for the friendship, fellowship, wisdom (both natural and prophetic); the bed; and not the least, the Pelican.

To my BCV friends who stood with, encouraged, prayed for, and anointed me—thank you!

To my old Adelaide friends who loved me, took me in, and journeyed with me in grace and forgiveness—with love and gratitude from an old friend. Blessing and honor in Jesus our Lord.

To Tina Maree's side of the family: Barry (in glory) and Anna, Jodie and Scott, Keith, (Nonno and Nonna), the family who took me in when I fell in love with your daughter, sister, and granddaughter—for the family you are, for which I have become a part, thank you and bless you. Most of all, may you come to know your Creator, Savior, and greatest treasure—Jesus!

To those friends not mentioned by name, believers, and yet-to-be believers—thank you for your love, encouragement, and support. Bless you in the reality of he who is "the way and the truth and the life" (John 14:6).

To the spiritual children who have come (and sometimes gone) and with whom we have shared, grown, prayed, and cried—may God, our Father, pour out his love and peace on you in Jesus, your Savior and Lord.

To the church—the members of Jesus' body—with whom we have traveled, are yet to, and will on that great day, "May the God of hope fill you with all joy and peace as you trust in him, so that you may overflow with hope by the power of the Holy Spirit" (Romans 15:13).

To the "great cloud of witnesses" (Hebrews 12:1) on the edge of their seats (as it were, without a drop of anxiety) and cheering us on, marveling at the unfolding glory of the Lord, for which they with grace and by faith pioneered the way in following "the pioneer and perfecter of our faith" (Hebrews 12:1)—I look forward to spending eternity in Jesus' glory with you.

To the angels, who in their love for and devotion to the Lord have ministered and minister God's unfailing love and grace to me—thank you so much, my (and the church's) precious and often undetected fellow servants (Hebrews 1:14; Revelation 19:10, 22:9).

Introduction

Many are the influences upon us personally and corporately throughout life from the word *go!* Remarkable also is the impact of discovering the unique character and value of each of our lives.

To say the least, God's kingdom, creation, handiwork, and sovereignty are, from sunrise to sunrise, astonishing to the point of being hard to believe.

We are yet still awaking, as the Lord's people, to the seamless relationship and closeness that exists between the spiritual and natural realms.

At this beachhead for the church as described in this book, where we are as his chosen people and go in the dawning of the day at hand, we need courage, courage, and more courage. Yes, "Be strong and very courageous" (Joshua 1:7).

Throughout this book, I repeat some parts. This is a necessary step to help equip you with a solid understanding of the heart and message of it.

Finally, and as truly as it ever has been, the Lord's "power is made perfect in weakness" (2 Corinthians 12:9).

"By the grace of God I am what I am, and his grace to me was not without effect" (1 Corinthians 15:10).

Chapter 1

He Makes Winds His Messengers

I was already well-acquainted with the Spirit of God stirring me in this way. It was right at 1:00 in the middle of the night in early 2003 that I was woken. I got out of bed and sat before the Lord, and I waited on him in the stillness and quietness of that night in our home in Tasmania.

I could not have foreseen the inestimable value of being obedient to this prompting. The insight in Scripture I was summoned to see and the value of the dream I was to then have far outweighed by a long shot what it took to overcome tiredness and leave the comfort of my bed.

During the early hours of that morning, I was drawn to read Acts 6-7. This account of Stephen's spirit and witness caught my attention at a level and in a way I had not encountered before. Here was a man who, like his Lord, was opposed and attacked by those who, as Jesus said such would believe, were "offering a service to God" (John 16:2-3).

Throughout Scripture and since the days of the early church, it has been revealed and seen that a religious spirit strongly resists and opposes change, in our hearts personally and in our lives corporately, through the moving of the Holy Spirit. Self-righteousness, pride, fear, human-made tradition, and inflexible structures are hallmarks of this spirit. The need to control for fear of not being in control is at its root.

Stephen's life, humility of heart, and dependence on the Spirit portray a stark contrast to what he encountered of this other spirit in those who were meant to know and represent God. The Holy Spirit has begun to, and will increasingly, draw the church's attention to this battle in these last days.

As in Acts 6-7 with the early church, so now the Lord is, and will yet, vividly expose the differences in spirit brought to light with this contention toward and against "the Way" (Acts 9:2; 19:9, 23; 24:14, 22). This extraordinary story is a sobering, exciting, and prophetic eye-opener to what is being exposed in and to the church and the world in these days.

Without a doubt, a considerable part of the church has been unaware of how much this adverse spirit has influenced and impacted the Lord's body and its strength. The Holy Spirit is at work that we would see this, placing light on what is incompatible with and contrary to the nature of Jesus' lordship and grace. Everything that can be shaken is being shaken so that what cannot be shaken remains—first and foremost in his church.

Stephen's life exemplifies the true power of the church and where the battle line of its freedom in Christ is drawn. It is both inevitable and telling when those demonstrating Stephen's integrity by walking in step with the Spirit of God are confronted with a spirit masquerading to be doing the same, yet "having a form of godliness but denying its power" (2 Timothy 3:5).

As I sat before the Lord, reading this part of Acts, the distinction and separation between these two very different spirits that govern people—even exceptional men and women who are zealous for God—was remarkable to see. Stephen, distinguished and set apart from those who contended with him, embodied what it is to be and what opposes one "known to be full of the Spirit and wisdom ... full of faith and of the Holy Spirit ... man full of God's grace and power" (Acts 6:3, 5, 8).

Extraordinarily, Stephen's "brothers and fathers" (Acts 7:2) could not receive what God spoke and revealed through him about their history, past and present, with the veil of another spirit covering their hearts, even though "All who were sitting in the Sanhedrin looked intently at Stephen, and they saw that his face was like the face of an angel" (Acts 6:15).

The messengers that God had sent and whom Stephen spoke about to his brothers and fathers, Stephen himself personified as a tangible example of a living instrument and mouthpiece of God. As such, in his concluding remarks, Stephen announced fearlessly with the love of Christ, of their negligence and ignorance about the ways of the Spirit, declaring, "You stiff-necked people! Your hearts and ears are still uncircumcised. You are just like your ancestors: You always resist the Holy Spirit!" (Acts 7:51)

The Changing Landscape

I was so deeply absorbed and impacted as I read, as though watching on as a live witness, that when I finally finished, having read from Acts 6:1 through 8:3, it was 4:00 a.m. Where did the time go? Time and place in the realm of the Spirit can be very different than what it is like in the realm of the natural we are accustomed to.

Tired, I went back to bed and went out like a light. No sooner had I gone to sleep than I found myself in a dream. I woke up in the dream from the same depth of sleep I had just fallen into. I was the front seat passenger in the car of an old friend, and while "Sir" John was driving, I began to sit up by adjusting the seat upright.

After a roundabout journey, we arrived at a beach. I got out of the car and stood looking down along the beach from my elevated vantage point. (My longtime friend went off elsewhere.)

This beach was very familiar to me! I had known it well from a young age. However, its landscape had changed. Nevertheless, I could still recognize it as the same beach. What makes a beach a beach, and a familiar one at that, hadn't changed—just how it looked had.

I saw heavy machinery down on the beach. Men sought to return the landscape to how it had been. They worked hard at it. The level of activity reflected their determination and matched the sense of just how much they did this in their own strength. Theirs was clearly an uphill battle and a fight they could not win with the extent of the change that had occurred. Their blindness to seeing this was evident in their misplaced focus.

That they preferred and were secure with only what they knew could explain this, given that the beach was still the beach. Different as it was, it still had the wonderful sense about a beach that draws us and makes us appreciate and value what is so unique and life-giving about it.

As I observed this scene, I sensed the fear of the Lord come upon me unlike that which I had known to that point in my life or since. To describe it is difficult. Suffice to say that I experienced God's presence, power, holiness, majesty, authority, and sovereignty in my spirit and in the atmosphere.

With this, I felt irresistibly persuaded to look out to sea. I was stunned by what I saw. The very nature of what had brought about the altered landscape of the beach previously was obvious. I saw many, many winds. These whirlwinds were very powerful. They were not a great distance out and were clearly moving toward the beach.

I somehow knew that just one of these winds was responsible for the change so far. Seeing what was yet to come and knowing this was of God meant that this change was but a small measure and deposit toward what was yet to come and had to have good reason and great purpose. It was even more obvious that to resist these winds and their intention was nothing short of foolishness.

Seeing, sensing, and experiencing this profound, prophetic scene with the fear of the Lord on me, I then backed well away from being associated in any way with or being a party to resisting the nature, work, and ways of the Holy Spirit. At this, I awoke from the dream!

The Grace of God

The connection was more than apparent! The beach symbolically represents the church. In the days of Stephen and the early church, God re-landscaped what represented his kingdom. As then, so now! The reason for the need for this, and the subsequent conflict, remains to this day and is being highlighted.

Compelled as I am to write this book, I am very conscious and aware, by the Spirit, that these winds described are upon the church. With good reason and great purpose, "He makes winds his messengers" (Psalm 104:4).

Where the church walks in step with and by the power of the Spirit, like Stephen, it reflects and exemplifies Jesus in the flesh as members of his body—as the church. Where on the other hand the church is out of step with truly knowing the Lord as the Lord would be known, it will find itself repeating history—and not for the first time—by doing the opposite of what it professes while not seeing it.

It is a sign in itself of where we are when the grace that we found in Jesus is not the fullness of the grace we walk in, either personally or corporately. Yet it is by the grace of God that we would be blessed to even see this, in order that we would turn and look to the Lord afresh. In this, the humility of Christ returns to the church!

The love of Christ that we knew at first is the love we come back to, and even greater than it was. The cross of Jesus, power of his resurrection, and their reality in and through the members of his body, as they are in Scripture (in Acts as much as anywhere), are at the heart of the necessity for this extraordinary change.

The remarkable thing about the Lord's unfailing love for us is that he would revive us and awaken us to build (and rebuild where necessary) upon the only foundation—the cornerstone—the Lord Jesus. With humility and meekness of heart, we must see that we have made grace (Spirit) law (flesh) with much of what we do as church. We may well be shocked to see with new eyes in this context that "The law was brought in that the trespass might increase. But where sin increased, grace increased all the more" (Romans 5:20).

In God's wisdom, we will yet see grace as it is intended to be and what it really looks like in and through the church. This is what will change the landscape. This is the purpose, as much as anything, for the winds. Their affect will not be as we might imagine. This shift is so dramatic that the time is coming when we will not recognize church as it was. Yet we will know it is the church, just as the beach is still a beach even though its landscape is significantly altered. This will also draw many into God's kingdom, because grace leads to life.

Where we have again gone back in our own strength to doing the very things Jesus died for and saved us from, he will, in his great love, demonstrate that his grace is greater than the law that we have succumbed to all over again. Indeed, the law will become the very means by which we see our need of God's amazing grace.

With good reason and great purpose, the winds of the Spirit are at hand to enable the church to see this. Whatever is not born of water and the Spirit will not stand. The day has surely come for "the removing of what can be shaken—that is, created things—so that what cannot be shaken may remain" (Hebrews 12:27).

Chapter 2

The Wisdom and Power of Humility

True humility and meekness of heart are the posture of where our relationships with and lives in Christ begin. This wisdom is where we are called to remain in our Lord Jesus, personally and corporately, until the end of the day. When the body of Christ deviates from the grace it has through this foundation, it is called to account. "God opposes the proud but shows favor to the humble" (James 4:6). Favor and grace are one and the same!

This wisdom and power of humility is returning to the church! The very nature and heart of our Creator, Savior, and Lord—Jesus—is being revealed in a renewed way. This is a revival and fresh awakening of the reality of the kingdom of God, in the cross and resurrection of Jesus, in and among the members of his body—Jesus in the flesh in us.

What true relationship, peace, unity, and oneness with God and one another really looks like is being brought to light. This comes at the expense of external appearances that belie and are contrary to the inward and living reality of "Christ in us" (Colossians 1:27).

The church will see what the church and "church" are missing. This is in order that we would see and know what the church really is. "You are a chosen people, a royal priesthood, a holy nation, God's special possession, that you may declare the praises of him who called you out of darkness into his wonderful light" (1 Peter 2:9).

The church is being realigned by the Spirit with the same power and boldness the early church experienced and embodied. The Holy Spirit will do this, preceding Jesus' return, in order to manifest the tangible reality of the kingdom "on earth as it is in heaven" (Matthew 6:10). Read "on earth" as "in us" "as it is in heaven."

Light, life, and truth are on the march! Consequently, any form of pride or ungodly fear, contrary to the good news, is being exposed. Whatever has infiltrated and weakened the church is being made clear and known. This is about the final battle between light and darkness coming to its climax. "For it is time for judgment to begin with God's household; and if it begins with us, what will the outcome be for those who do not obey the gospel of God" (1 Peter 4:17).

The Church's Spiritual Battle

As described in chapter one, I was awakened during the night to engage in, through reading the Word of God, the conflict and hostility that Stephen encountered as we read it in Acts 6-7, which the Lord Jesus and the early church relentlessly, and to the death, faced.

This same spiritual battle is being fought out and has deeply impacted the members and parts of the body of Christ closer to home in the church than what we might like to believe. If this was the case for the early emerging church, as I will address, and with what was needed to awaken it to this reality, we are blessed to also see and contend with it and be refined as God's people in the process.

The dream I had on the back of this awakening during the night gave insight into and prophetically magnified Acts 6-7. The changes and ensuing conflict in those days, the church is likewise experiencing today.

In the dream, I saw winds of the Spirit poised to re-landscape the church to realign it with humility and resurrection power. These winds came following a deposit or taste of just one such wind. That initial wind resulted in a resistance in those unaware of God's good reason for it and great purpose in it. I will return later in the book to look at the wind in 1994 that was intended to prepare the church "for such a time as this" (Esther 4:14).

When the body of Christ—the "salt of the earth" and "light of the world" (Matthew 5:13-16)—is set in and bound by ways in which its security and life are in what is other than its cornerstone, it will be (and is indeed being) shaken. Where the church is, in its own strength, immovable, limited, and measured, this will change, "for God gives the Spirit without limit" (John 3:34).

The Lord is displacing the familiarity of tradition, structure, and the like where they are unyielding to his moving and greatness. He is exchanging fear, pride, and restriction within our lives personally and in his church corporately for the freedom and likeness of our Lord and his kingdom.

Our God does this in and through the church that it would know anew the living reality of the person and work of Jesus, the ways of the Spirit, relationship and intimacy with God, and what it means to be the dwelling of his presence and a house of prayer for all nations.

In an exciting though sobering way, the Lord is at work to expose the cause for this conflict against grace within the church personally and corporately. The church across the earth is being alerted through the moving of the Holy Spirit to one of its greatest adversaries to its freedom, its moving forward in step with the Spirit, and its maturity.

Resist, as this adverse and embedded religious spirit may to the winds upon us, it will not prevail against Jesus truly being Lord of his church and him building his church his way. "'For my thoughts are not your thoughts, neither are your ways my ways,' declares the LORD" (Isaiah 55:8).

Aligned with the Cornerstone

The spirit and power of Elijah are at hand—a preparing of the way for the Lord. Those who exalt themselves over others will be brought low. Those who are humble will be raised up. Where the way is not Jesus, it shall be straightened out and made accessible. Hearts will turn to where hearts are meant to be. The focus of the church will shift to what it has always intended to be aligned to.

The foundation of our salvation and lives will be restored. Our first love will return. Our Savior will be marveled at for just how wonderful his love and truly great his grace are. The glory of the Lord will be revealed. "Every valley shall be filled in, every mountain and hill made low. The crooked roads shall become straight, the rough ways smooth. And all people will see God's salvation" (Luke 3:4-6, quoting Isaiah 40:3-5).

The foundation and cornerstone on which the church is built, the Holy Spirit is recovering, restoring, renewing, and reviving. The members of Christ's body are being shaken, stirred, and awakened to "Arise, shine ..." (Isaiah 60:1-3). However, this is an unwelcome threat to what has sought to undermine the church's foundation, strength, and glorious purpose.

Our freedom fighter, the Lord Jesus, brought this undermining, opposing religious spirit vividly and graphically to light, unmasking and deflating its dominance. As it is recorded in Matthew 22:34 through the whole of Matthew 23, on the platform of his integrity as the Messiah, the Son of God, and the Son of Man, before the crowds, his disciples, and the silenced Pharisees, he wielded a piercing sword as "the Word of God" (Revelation 19:13).

Embodying the truth in himself as a living sacrifice, Jesus charged that the greatest among us would be those who served us. With a decisive blow for all time to inordinate pride and condescending superiority born of fear while with uplifting consolation to the gentle, meek, and humble in heart, he declared, "For those who exalt themselves will be humbled, and those who humble themselves will be exalted" (Matthew 23:12).

Under the constant measuring, questioning, and demand to conform, the religious spirit and its system, placed upon Jesus, collapsed when faced with the power of life, truth, humility, and liberty in him. It did not stand where he stood!

The Lord Jesus and the love he walked in are exceedingly and immeasurably greater than what sought to depose his kingdom.

> A rock was cut out, but not by human hands. It struck the statue on its feet of iron and clay and smashed them ... The wind swept them away without leaving a trace. But the rock that struck the statue became a huge mountain and filled the whole earth. (Daniel 2:34-35, in the context of Daniel 2)

When the members of Christ's body discern and confront that same religious spirit in the wisdom and power of humility, it will yield to the Lord in them. The stand that masquerading spirit has taken, where it has been accommodated, will collapse. It remains as it is only by virtue of our ignorance to its deceptive guise, in "having a form of godliness but denying its power" (2 Timothy 3:5).

The Spirit of Jesus is at hand to unmask the form without the power. In his love for his church, he will provide for us the grace and truth needed to see this and turn from it in order to turn to him.

Christ's power is at hand in the winds that blow, even as they blew as they did in the early church. These winds delivered Saul (Paul) and numerous others, even after salvation, from the legacy of the deceit of the Garden of Eden that Cain embellished and Abel overcame.

Chapter 3

As Then, So Now

A further extraordinary, revealing example and embodiment of the power of the good news of God's grace, along with Abel, is in Paul the apostle. As Saul prior to his radically transformed life, the contrast between living by a spirit of fear and pride and the freedom he found in God's grace is remarkable to say the least.

Saul came to experience, know, and pass on something greater by far than what had held him captive. What had purported to be godly in practice and at which he excelled but was based on a lie masquerading as the truth, when exposed and unmasked, was exchanged. As he could say it well, so mindful of its truth, "For the Spirit God gave us does not make us timid, but gives us power, love and self-discipline" (2 Timothy 1:7).

The Spirit of God and grace are life-giving and display the courage that David did before the armies of Israel, Goliath, and the Philistines (1 Samuel 17). Flesh, on the other hand, walks in fear and timidity and is cowardly in how it manifests. "Those who are victorious ... I will be their God and they will be my children. But the cowardly ... will be consigned to the fiery lake of burning sulfur" (Revelation 21:7-8). There are no cowards in the kingdom. This is sobering stuff!

A religious spirit—a spirit of fear—having its way in us and among us as the church (generally) for so long now, has cunningly intruded, cloaked as God, blinding us that this could not be true of those who represent and testify the opposite of such insecurity. The potential of this spirit's influence does not necessarily halt at the threshold of the church—until now!

Saul's fear, pride, blindness, and drive were governed and accompanied by the zeal rooted in this opposing religious spirit. This was insightfully evident at the time of the stoning of Stephen and the consequent persecution and scattering of the church, in which Saul was deeply and personally involved.

Note well that when anyone personally or corporately walks in what Saul did, even a Christian or fellowship of the Lord's people, thinking that they do a service for God, as Saul did, they become for those who truly walk by grace the strengthening (and the means of scattering) of that very grace (Acts 8:1).

In the years following Jesus' spectacular intervention and deliverance of Saul "out of darkness into his wonderful light" (1 Peter 2:9), this "chosen instrument" (Acts 9:15), through seasoned apostolic apprenticeship, suffering, and ministry, understood as well as anybody the nature of this resistant and ungracious religious spirit. Jesus referred to this spirit, saying, "The thief comes only to steal and kill and destroy." But of that which is of the Spirit of Jesus, he said, "I have come that they may have life, and have it to the full" (John 10:10).

In spelling out once more to the Galatians, this time in writing, about God's grace in separating Paul from his previous way of life and from his misguided extreme zeal, he spoke to these friends whom he loved and served with an unquenchable jealousy for the Lord and their welfare.

Paul was, as he put it, "astonished" (Galatians 1:6) by the way these brothers and sisters were impacted all over again—after salvation—by this old deceitful, subtle, and undermining spiritual adversary with its restless, works-driven, and flesh-pleasing spirit.

The subtle and divisive nature of this masquerading light seek to reestablish among the Lord's people the stronghold of the lie that says God is never satisfied and we are never good enough while demanding that we need to do something to prove our value and worth.

This deceptive darkness is diametrically opposed to the rest and peace we have by grace through faith in (the faithfulness of) Jesus. We can all identify with this propensity of the flesh to give room for and way to darkness. When our flesh, personally and corporately, is not yielded to the Spirit, it is unsettled and seeks to have us find, without ever finding, what God alone accomplished in Christ: our *rest* in being at home in and with the Lord, where we are, wherever that might be.

The Lord's people who truly live by grace are at home in who we are, in all our great diversity, because of Jesus—our Rock. The foundation determines the structure. The structure, well built, is as secure and strong as that which it is founded on.

When grace is grace, as much as it is for any one of us, and is also regarded as the same for all of us, we then begin to understand what it really looked like and will look like when "All the believers were together and had everything in common" (Acts 2:44). Likewise, the landscape of the church is remarkable to behold when together "We know that we have passed from death to life, because we love each other. Anyone who does not love remains in death" (1 John 3:14).

When we stand secure because we trust in and know Jesus, even when again facing what once held us to ransom through fear, the power of that old adversary will yield to the lordship of Jesus and the truth that "the one who is in you is greater than the one who is in the world" (1 John 4:4).

There Is No Fear in Love

It is remarkable to say the least that the Holy Spirit also had to speak in such strong terms through the apostle, not only to God's church generally about that old, ungracious bondage, but also to Peter, of all apostles—not only so, but even Barnabas! No amount of walking with the Lord and seeing his goodness and power exempts one from the possibility of coming under the pressure of this religious spirit and the fear it evokes.

As Paul testified to the churches with apostolic authority,

> When Cephas came to Antioch, I opposed him to his face, because he stood condemned. For before certain men came from James, he used to eat with the Gentiles. But when they arrived, he began to draw back and separate himself from the Gentiles because he was afraid of those who belonged to the circumcision group. The

13

other Jews joined him in his hypocrisy, so that by their hypocrisy even Barnabas was led astray. (Galatians 2:11-13)

There are two very noticeable and telling things about the hypocrisy rooted in this religious spirit that the apostle Paul exposes. Firstly, the progressive and divisive nature of slipping away from grace, in the way that Peter "began to draw back and separate himself." Secondly, this spirit brings fear, for "he was afraid." Fear unchecked leads to hypocrisy, given that "There is no fear in love, because fear has to do with punishment. The one who fears is not made perfect in love" (1 John 4:18).

Paul went on in speaking to the churches in Galatia, and through them to us, in unmasking this beast. Whenever the grace of God in Christ is diminished even an iota—the smallest jot or smidgen—we have, either personally or corporately, done the opposite to what we did when found grace in Jesus. The writer to the Hebrews did not mince words, declaring,

How much more severely do you think someone deserves to be punished who has trampled the Son of God underfoot, who has treated as an unholy thing the blood of the covenant that sanctified them, and has insulted the Spirit of grace? (Hebrews 10:29)

These words of warning are sobering words! The church must understand that anything that eclipses grace being grace and takes precedence over the Spirit of grace—the Holy Spirit—is idolatry. Jesus died and rose again to deliver us from this very thing. It is very possible for believers to succumb to this intimidating nature of another god. As John appealed as a final word in his letter to believers as family, "Dear children, keep yourselves from idols" (1 John 5:21).

Above All Else

God and his ways must be loved and obeyed above all else. Indeed, we cannot truly love another or others without loving his Son, which is evidenced in loving as Jesus loves. Our evangelism will explode when we truly walk in "As I have loved you, so you must love one another. By this everyone will know that you are my disciples, if you love one another" (John 13:34-35). This looks like showing another the very grace we have received. We love the Father and the Son, as much as in anything, by displaying the grace we have been shown by God to another in whatever way we have received it.

Deliverance from idolatry—no longer loving anything or anyone else more than the Lord (while loving like the Lord)—should be a primary sign of the grace and power of God that the church lives in and by. When this is true beyond question and evident in practice, then the testimony of Jesus in our lives would burst forth with that same effect it's had on us upon others.

We are incredibly blessed to have the Holy Spirit reveal this to us and to see the contrast between grace and a religious spirit for what it is. This is simply yet profoundly God in his faithfulness giving us more grace.

> Or do you think Scripture says without reason that he jealously longs for the spirit he has caused to dwell in us? But he gives us more grace. That is why Scripture says: "God opposes the proud but shows favor to the humble" … humble yourselves before the Lord, and he will lift you up. (James 4:5-6, 10)

This grace to see where we are—and in this, where we shouldn't be—humbles us anew, and we do what we did at the outset. We turn to (repent) and look to the Lord. His blood alone will atone for even the very thing we say we believe yet don't truly walk in. Seeing where we are and where we shouldn't be is a wake-up call!

The least measure of drawing back or looking down on another or others is contrary to wisdom and the good news on which our salvation is based. Keeping our relational compass aligned with the efficacy of the blood of Jesus is a plumb line anchored to the cornerstone of our faith. Our spiritual eyes are being refocused. Our identities in the cross of Christ, power of his resurrection, and glory of his ascension as Lord over all will yet blaze afresh across the nations. Humility, faith, and glory go hand in hand!

Mere Flesh

The law (without the Spirit), drawing strength from mere flesh, opens the door to another spirit other than the Holy Spirit. Unchecked and undiscerned, this religious spirit governs our way. In wisdom and patience, the true Lord of the church has determined, as he did with Peter, Barnabas, and the Galatians, that these things should happen up to a point.

As then, so now, the Spirit is actively and intentionally at work and moving to reveal the reality of our condition. Make no mistake; it was in love for Jesus and the members of his body that Paul, compelled as he was, spoke up about Peter and Barnabas' backtracking. In no lesser terms does the Spirit speak to the church today.

> When I saw that they were not acting in line with the truth of the gospel ... a person is not justified by the works of the law, but by faith in Jesus Christ ... For through the law I died to the law so that I might live for God. I have been crucified with Christ and I no longer live, but Christ lives in me. The life I now live in the body, I live by faith in the Son of God, who loved me and gave himself for me. I do not set aside the grace of God, for if righteousness could be gained through the law, Christ died for nothing! (Galatians 2:14–21).

The whole point of the Messiah's love, sacrifice, and death is at the core of everything for the church from here till Jesus returns. Yes, it always has been; however, the grace of God will come to light not only as good as it ever has, but also greater in glory and better than it ever has.

The fear of the Lord, love of the Lord, and love for the Lord will produce this! The humility and meekness of the church, in whatever form(s) they will take, will become the world's greatest evangelical event. Our postures will be like those of our Lord, his servant Stephen, his servant Paul, and the one whom Jesus loved, John, on the Island of Patmos (Revelation 1:9-10).

Witchcraft

It must be understood that this religious spirit is a spirit that, shocking to have revealed and puzzling perhaps to understand (as it will be to many), is also a spirit of witchcraft. Difficult as it is to swallow, often enough witchcraft has had its way among us.

As Paul said in the context to which we have spoken with the calculated incision of a surgeon's knife and the bluntness of a deeply concerned friend, "You foolish Galatians! Who has bewitched you? ... Are you so foolish? After beginning by means of the Spirit, are you now trying to finish by means of the flesh?" (Galatians 3:1-3).

Whatever we do by means of the flesh and call church, fellowship, worship, unity, a message, etc., we have not done, as we did at the beginning, by the Spirit. How amazing are God's grace and forbearance that he would remain so faithful when his own heart so deeply grieves while we limp along when we should bound along. The glory we've lost will not only be the glory we'll regain as we humble ourselves or are humbled, but truly, the latter glory will also be greater than the former.

Acting in accordance to a spirit other than the Holy Spirit to manipulate, dominate, or control others in whatever unwitting, subtle, or flagrant guise and form that might be done is witchcraft. A religious spirit and witchcraft are one and the same. None of us is immune to its potential effect or to being a party to it except by the veracity of the blood of Jesus.

It is Jesus' blood by which we are victorious, and it is far more powerful, even in the face of our unawareness or awareness, of stepping by a spirit other than the Holy Spirit. The Spirit of life in us protects and cleanses us from the spirit of death in what we might entertain. To this we are being awakened!

As then (at the outset church), so now (for the end time church), the testimony and proclamation will be, as much as anything, "Christ has set us free to live a free life. So take your stand! Never again let anyone put a harness of slavery on you" (Galatians 5:1 MSG).

17

Chapter 4

Outside the Camp

By adding significant insight to this age-old contention warring against the church, the writer of Hebrews, with exceptional understanding and fatherly love, addressed the church. They uprooted the lies of deception burrowing into the hearts of believers and redirected the Lord's embattled people to fix their thoughts and eyes on Jesus—the Son of God—above all else.

In reinforcing faith and rest in Jesus' sacrifice for sins, this writer and shepherd sought to circumvent this persuasive proneness of believers to drift from grace and toward a reversal of the foundation of our salvation and spiritual maturity. Summoning God's people with the solution and antidote, we also hear what the Spirit implores once more regarding our Lord Jesus: "Let us, then, go to him outside the camp, bearing the disgrace that he bore" (Hebrews 13:13).

There is a renewed and revived calling and summons for what it is for us, as believers today, to be with Jesus on the outside. What it is to be truly set apart and called outside the camp—knowing and walking with our Lord and having his humility—is as much as anything the good reason and great purpose for the winds coming upon the church. Indeed, the church (*ekklesia* in New Testament Greek) means "called out."

Like Simon Peter, Saul, the great cloud of witnesses gone before, and every true believer to this day until kingdom come in all its fullness, Jesus calls us "out of darkness into his wonderful light" (1 Peter 2:9-10). This is a visible (out in the open) and deeply relational place. It is where the Lord meets us and we meet him in his light. To be inside the camp, on the other hand, is to be where we do not see or recognize God and one another as he is and as we are to be truly known.

The embodiment of the new covenant is outside the camp. As Paul put it so insightfully, "written not with ink but with the Spirit of the living God, not on tablets of stone, but on tablets of human hearts ... not of the letter but of the Spirit; for the letter kills, but the Spirit gives life" (2 Corinthians 3:3-6).

The Scripture is truth in as much as the truth lives (is alive) in us. This is what it is to see a true form of godliness with power (the power of the Spirit). To be inside the camp is to be where there is a form (structure) that is based on appearances—what it appears to be—but is not the reality of what it claims to be. The Pharisees personified this, and the church does when it does as they did. Their form of godliness (and our form like theirs) disempowers relationships both with God and others. It puts God at a distance!

Religion (a form without the power of God) sets itself above and not alongside. The Holy Spirit came, as Jesus said, like him as "another advocate to help you and be with you forever" (John 14:16). The context of true godliness and righteousness (what is right in God's sight) is relationship—God drawing near to us and us drawing near to God.

Intimacy with God

The first and notable mention in Scripture of the phrase "outside the camp" is found in the context of Exodus 33:7-11. "Now Moses used to take a tent and pitch it outside the camp some distance away, calling it the 'tent of meeting.' Anyone enquiring of the LORD would go to the tent of meeting outside the camp" (Exodus 33:7).

"Outside the camp" here represents where the Lord is and dwells. It is where we have turned to him, sought him out, and found intimacy with God. It is a deeply relational place of the heart for each of us personally and all of us corporately. It is also where God's people find wisdom and insight.

The source of life and hope is "outside the camp." As David put it, "I sought the LORD, and he answered me; he delivered me from all my fears. Those who look to him are radiant; their faces are never covered with shame" (Psalm 34:4-5; see also 1 Peter 2:6).

This closeness and oneness with the Lord in the way that Moses and Joshua experienced (among others) and the disciples knew so intimately both preceding and following Jesus' ascension—at whatever the cost— are at heart and in spirit what being outside the camp means.

Such closeness and oneness with God "outside the camp" are seen where "The LORD would speak to Moses face to face, as one speaks to a friend" (Exodus 33:11). The disciples experienced the same in following and being with Jesus. Every believer has been given this grace and access and has this right as a child of God as a son or daughter of the King of kings. This is what it is to truly know our God as he would have us know him. To know him in this way is to know both the fear of the Lord and the love of God—in Jesus, by the Spirit.

Bearing the Disgrace

Outside the camp is also where we suffer because of the environment and culture in which we live in this world that are hostile to the light and glory of the kingdom of God. We suffer like our Lord Jesus, as the early church, the disciples, Stephen, Paul, and John (in Revelation) did.

These sufferings of Christ and our suffering in Christ bring forth life to the world. Just as Herod felt threatened and tried to kill Jesus in his infancy in order to prevent the maturity of Immanuel, so the body of the Messiah is threatened, and suffering occurs as it comes into its maturity in Christ being formed in us.

Prophetically, as with our Lord, so with his body in our obedience and intercession:

> During the days of Jesus' life on earth, he offered up prayers and petitions with fervent cries and tears to the one who could save him from death, and he was heard because of his reverent submission. Son though he was, he learned obedience from what he suffered and, once made perfect, he became the source of eternal salvation for all who obey him and was designated by

God to be a high priest in the order of Melchizedek.
(Hebrews 5:7-10)

The birth, infancy, and maturity of the body of Christ come with
suffering outside the camp. When we go to Jesus—the tree of life—and
remain in and with him, away from what we were delivered from inside
the camp of the flesh—the tree of the knowledge of good and evil—we
bear the disgrace that he bore.

We can be outside the camp inside the camp. However, that which
is inside the camp will react to what is not of it unless you compromise.
But whom do we love more than all else? Do we love a form of
godliness? Or do we love the power of God in what he has done to
deliver us out of that very bondage of needing to do something in
particular in order to be justified rather than to trust in Jesus' sacrifice?

Real

Our understanding of church is in for extraordinary transformation.
It will yet be as real as the Lord himself—indeed, even more real than
what we think of as reality. What this looks like is about both the
natural and spiritual being seamlessly connected and our being at home
in who we truly are in Jesus. We will know, by the Spirit, the spirit of
the real meaning of "And God raised us up with Christ and seated us
with him in the heavenly realms in Christ Jesus" (Ephesians 2:6).

Being outside the camp is both natural and spiritual. It is the most
inviting place to be. The presence of the Lord attracts both believers
and those who do not yet believe. That attraction is God in who he is
as the One to be known and desired more than all else. The life coming
from him and his ways is far more attractive than the death of our ways
without him.

It is not what we do that we call church that counts. It is who Jesus
is, what he has done, and what he is doing that make us the church, the
salt of the earth and the light of the world. We are either attracted to
or repelled by Jesus coming in a form we do not recognize. Therefore,
we must truly know the Holy Spirit. Remember, "This is the verdict:
Light has come into the world, but people loved darkness instead of

light because their deeds were evil" (John 3:19). This applies also to what is of a religious spirit that fights tooth and nail to be kept from being exposed for what it really is. It does not invite transparency. Nevertheless, the distinction between what is of God and outside the camp and what is not of the Holy Spirit and inside the camp of religion, even in us, is at hand.

At the end of the day, there will be two distinctively different people. There will be those who are blindly under the control of a religious spirit and never really at rest and those who walk by the Spirit in freedom and peace. "And you will again see the distinction between the righteous and the wicked, between those who serve God and those who do not" (Malachi 3:18).

The landscape of the church can dramatically change without fear for how that looks, for the substance will still be there. It is no different than what stares at us in the face all the time in one another. Church, as we think of it, can look very different from one gathering to the next—indeed, as different as we are! Such are the members of the body of the Lord. Just as we can be at home with and love the diversity in creation itself, how much more with our Creator and his creativity with the church?

Yes, doing church can be as diverse in how it looks as we all are. We are each a powerful expression and part of the grace of God. When the Spirit is truly Lord, church can potentially look as diverse as the body itself, with our being as at home with diversity as family is in the natural.

Coming of Age

All of us, without exception, are in for a change in the way we see the Lord and ourselves that completely removes any notion of or room for pride and arrogance. With this change afoot and its reflection of God's kingdom, we are coming of age—the age to come! Yes, the church will walk in having "tasted the goodness of the word of God and the powers of the age to come" (Hebrews 6:5).

The church will be as "living and active as any double edged sword" (Hebrews 4:12), because the Word of God himself lives in us and through us. Scripture will be as powerful as it is intended to be. It will be living Scripture in and among us, as it was at any stage written in Scripture.

It makes every bit of sense that the church will be seen and walk in the love and grace of Jesus, as it is to see Jesus. We could well call this the body language of Jesus. As John, our brother and companion in the suffering and kingdom and patient endurance that are ours in Jesus, said, "This is how we know we are in him: Whoever claims to live in him must walk as Jesus did" (1 John 2:5-6).

If the Word of God himself and what is in the Word of God is in us, then what is in us will be as it was in Scripture. The reality of Jesus will be manifest in the flesh—in his body. Of this, we can be sure as we, by the Spirit, arise and shine. This is about the glory of God! Just as he has so wonderfully saved us, that very love and power—his glory—will shine through us. This is the testimony of Jesus in its power—the power of testimony—to do for others what it has done in us.

How did we stray from what the early church experienced with Jesus never leaving or forsaking it through the presence and power of the Spirit? Isn't it meant to be the same for us? Shouldn't that then look like Jesus being with us as he was with the disciples, in no lesser way, and in an even greater way?

A form of godliness without the power, on the other hand, weakens us and dilutes the gospel when we conform to it. It does not empower; it diminishes. Understand, then, that compromise with the form is exposed to enable us to see these things.

We shoot ourselves in the foot whenever we think less of another member (Christ in us) as much as we believe Jesus loves us personally. Those kinds of prideful and arrogant thoughts have no place in the church as a reflection of Jesus in the flesh—his body. Again, any distinction between what we say we believe and reality will be humbled.

A Corporate David

The Spirit of Jesus is blowing, and will yet be as the wind of no small storm, blowing (breathing) on his church to bring us to our finest hour. We will arise and shine without the pride that has infiltrated our ranks through this religious spirit that has held us back. Whatever delays there have been, and resistance to this movement of the Holy Spirit, by that which is not of the Spirit, is for fear and terror that Jesus is going to be seen again in the flesh through his body—the church.

Like David before Goliath, the church living in heart outside the camp will contend with the same defiant voice against the army of the living God. With its hostility, fear mongering, and rage, either veiled or exposed, Goliath will more than meet his match in the gentle, bold, and courageous corporate David running toward the now drawn battle line.

No amount of resistance will deter those God has aligned (and is aligning) with his kingdom. Be aware that how one may look is not what is most important. Remember, even the man of God, Samuel, as close in relationship as he was to the Lord, needed to see that "the LORD does not look at the things people look at. People look at the outward appearance, but the LORD looks at the heart" (1 Samuel 16:7).

Everything that can be shaken is being shaken. We are being awakened to see that when the form or landscape of church has become our security or lens by which we see the kingdom, then idolatry and flesh have become lord.

Therefore, when the Sovereign Lord sees our folly and blindness, he shakes us and awakens us, as he does in his love and jealousy, away from a form of godliness back to (toward) his power. Young David (as with Stephen) typified this power! The source of David's power was that he truly knew God and put his trust in the God he knew.

The exposure and eviction of a spirit in the church other than the Spirit of the Lord being Lord is on the march. The Spirit must be Lord! It is only by the Holy Spirit that Jesus is lifted up, glorified, and all people are drawn to him. We must know the Spirit who makes Jesus and what is of Jesus known.

As Jesus himself said of the Spirit,

> When he, the Spirit of truth, comes, he will guide you into all truth. He will not speak on his own; he will speak only what he hears, and he will tell you what is yet to come. He will glorify me because it is from me that he will receive what he will make known to you ...

the Spirit will receive from me what he will make
known to you. (John 16:12-15)

Yes, discerning by what spirit we do what we do is a reason why
the winds are here to shake all that can be shaken. Often enough to
date, until now, the spirit of religion has either gone undetected through
its subtle and hidden influence or simply been welcome as though
this form of church is the Lord. Truly, exposure of the vast difference
between a religious spirit and the Spirit of Jesus is at hand!

The church that knows its Lord is moving toward and going "to
him outside the camp, bearing the disgrace he bore" (Hebrews 13:13).

Chapter 5

The Storm Front

The intense and immense storm approaching covered the entire distant horizon. In this dream, my three-year-old son (at the time), Samuel, was with me in the car when I saw it. There was a deep and compelling sense that we should take refuge in the familiar place I had known throughout my life.

"Familiar place"—does this sound familiar? Yes, it was the church, as many of us have known it as we have grown up. Taking refuge there, however, meant heading straight toward the storm front, where the opposing pressures in the atmosphere were greatest.

Still some distance from church and while on the way, I caught sight of and heard something that took hold of me and got my attention. I observed this whole following scene in a way which somewhat resembled a scene caught in slow-motion.

Looking to my right as I drove, I saw a rural setting. A house was set back on a property. But it was the land on both sides and in front of this home that captured my attention. To say that things on the property were messy would be a way to describe it. The word that came to mind was *debris*. Things weren't clean and tidy!

I then saw people. They raked, tidied, and cleaned up. It took work to do this, but they were clearly resolutely determined. The most notable thing about the sense of these people and this scene was the life and peace in and about them. They were not anxious! Contrary to what you might expect with the kind of mess they were in, they were completely calm.

This made me think of the Scriptures. "In repentance and rest is your salvation, in quietness and trust is your strength" (Isaiah 30:15). "The fruit of that righteousness will be peace; its effect will be quietness and confidence forever" (Isaiah 32:17). With this coming from them and in the atmosphere about them, I was inwardly drawn toward this place in a way that increased as I continued to watch.

There was no doubt that these represented those who look to the Lord no matter how messy things are and with whatever debris their lives have caused, whether that was for reasons of being religious beforehand or walking in whatever darkness they may have, whether before coming to the Lord or since having been born again. They knew what to do—repent—in order to make way for the Lord. What they did was not their salvation. It was a consequence of the amazing grace they knew in their hearts. That's the sense I had about them and what I could identify for myself as one with them.

No sooner had they done a good job of making their unattractive dwelling place appear appealing and desirable than it became even more so as grass began to grow on this land. It grew faster than it would normally or could in the natural. I saw irrigation equipment being used, making use of what they had. Then a steady, solid, good rain began falling. This outpouring turned the field into lush and flourishing grass.

This whole scene as a prophetic picture of the grace of God at work in and upon believers who were without pretenses was heartwarming and insightful. Then, overlaying this scene, before Samuel and I moved on toward the storm front, an image of the face of a man of God I knew was magnified on the screen of my spirit.

This brother in the Lord repeatedly made a statement that emphasized being God-fearing and following God in everything. A Scripture that accurately conveys the spirit of what he said is, "I have found David son of Jesse, a man after my own heart; he will do everything I want him to do" (Acts 13:22).

Our Place?

Encouraged with an understanding of what this friend and brother communicated, I drove on. Soon Samuel and I arrived at the old, good, and familiar that I had been accustomed to throughout my life. However, the hope that there was safety in the familiar was soon to take a back seat. The distinction between what I was about to encounter, which I had not till then seen, with what I knew so well, against what I had just seen, experienced, and had communicated to me was truly insightful, sobering, and awakening.

Samuel and I came to a very grand old structure. This building appeared to me from the outside to look somewhat like Flinders Street Railway Station in Melbourne, Australia. Google it, and you will soon get a picture of what the building looked like. (Melbourne is the city in which I was born, bred, and spent most of my earlier years.)

We entered this grand old building. The structure covered and had within it familiar church denominations and fellowships that are among mainstream churches. In the dream, this center was, at one and the same time, a commuter railway station, terminus, and meeting place, just like Flinders Street Station.

It had different ramps that were the access ways to the platforms. From these, like any station, the train takes you to your destination or brings you from your departure point. Nevertheless, this Grand Central Station was the hub of what prophetically represented church.

When I sought to make our way by leading the way down a platform that I understood to be our church, we were literally barred from access. I attempted to squeeze my way through the obstructive structure at the entrance of the platform. The way was narrower than and different from the way Jesus surely meant when he said, "Enter through the narrow gate" (Matthew 7:13).

Realizing that I couldn't lead the way for my young son, I thought that I would at least let him attempt to find a way to what was intended to mirror freedom. Desiring him to know the Lord and be a valued member of the body of Christ, I thought that he would at least have the best likelihood, being that much smaller (and younger), to find the way.

It was difficult to watch him, much as he enthusiastically tried, seeking to work his way through the bars that inhibited his entry and blocked such childlike access. I understood with a renewed perspective the Scripture, "When Jesus saw this, he was indignant. He said to them, 'Let the little children come to me, and do not hinder them, for the kingdom of heaven belongs to such as these'" (Matthew 19:14, Mark 10:14, Luke 18:14).

With this, I thought that perhaps it would be easier to try a different ramp (church). Of the two other attempts we made, the story was the same. Whichever way we sought to take, rather than enabling us to walk in and enter in with freedom, liberty, and comfort, it was severely restrictive at best and imprisoning at worst. These were not the gospel and grace I knew!

As I stood there, wondering what would be best to do and which other platform we might try to access, we saw a man dressed in a way that without any mistake was a religious church leader. His appearance or form was what is identified as representing Christianity; yet his demeanor exuded a spirit of control and manipulation. He pointed (and you might even say herded) us to what he regarded as our place.

This proved to be no different than any other restrictive gateway we had experienced specifically as well as the sense of the whole place generally. It was not an easy reality to swallow. I had recognized this structure as the place in which I had been nurtured in my faith. I could not have been where I am today without it.

Somewhere along the way, the life of this old and familiar place had dulled. What had been good about it was now overshadowed by something other than what it was intended to be. What had been strength and served us very well once had now become resistant and disheartening.

Where we found ourselves was no longer truly and authentically embracing. The depth of love that was my experience of relationship with the Lord Jesus was not there. An unwelcome change of heart had occurred that brought a deep sense of grief to my soul and spirit.

The contrast in spirit between what I saw on our way and this place in which I was once so familiar could not have been starker. Here, where I was intuitively drawn and I thought we would be very much at home and safe, I was shaken to the core.

Added to this was the unsettled sense in the atmosphere with the impending intense storm front. Clearly, bearing down upon this structure, as I lift my head up even now as I write and pause to soak this all up again and be still before the Lord about it and the gravity of it all, I listen. I hear winds, and I sense movement.

A New Day

The Lord's people across the earth have heard afresh from the Spirit over a number of years that it is a new day for the church. The Spirit has heralded to our hearts a particular Word in the face of the limits and restrictions that have caused such heartache while serving great purpose in preparing us for walking without measure in Jesus' love and grace. That Word of God has been to "Forget the former things; do not dwell on the past. See, I am doing a new thing! Now it springs up; do you not perceive it?" (Isaiah 43:18-19).

In early 2003, I arrived home late on a Sunday evening with Tina Maree (my wife) and our son, Samuel, after having been to a gathering of the Lord's people in Smithton on the top end of Tasmania's northwest coast. At that time, we lived about forty minutes away, by car, from Smithton.

Earlier that evening, at the gathering of believers we attended known as Hands to the Plow, a brother in the Lord who wasn't one of the speakers shared a compelling prophetic picture that he was given the evening before. Simply put, Rodney was shown a scene in which there was a setting sun. He sensed fear with this ending of a day only to then realize, comforted, that it preceded the dawning of another day. He was given to know that what was setting was bringing about a new day!

As Tina Maree put two-year-old Samuel to bed, without realizing at first what I was doing, I fixed a bowl of cereal. (It is always an interesting experience to be somewhere before you wake up to where you are.) As I stood there in the kitchen, eating breakfast, Tina Maree came back out of Samuel's room and lovingly posed the question, "What are you doing?"

Her question struck me with the unusual strength you hear when a question is posed and you know that it is more than the person himself or herself asking. The Lord got me to ask what I was doing! He did this in the way that the Lord answers the question for you with the help of the Holy Spirit. It dawned on me that I was doing what you do at the outset of a new day.

The place in which I found myself in those moments awoke in me a sense of an even deeper awareness of the weight of importance about what Rodney had received. As I stood there with my breakfast bowl at the end of a day, the force of what was being conveyed to the church struck me. This has long stayed with me! Coupled with the other insights in this book, tallied with what many others also hear and see, the megaphone of heaven is on and to be taken notice of. Yes, we are at the setting of the day that is passing, and it holds no fear, for we are at the dawning of a new and glorious day for the church.

Again, even as the Lord has said to so many across the church over these years in many and various ways, the corporate kingdom's call at this time and in these days remains. Yes, I repeat this often enough throughout the book for good reason. The church is being summoned to "Arise, Shine, for your light has come, and the glory of the LORD rises upon you. See, darkness covers the earth and thick darkness is over the peoples, but the LORD rises upon you and his glory appears over you" (Isaiah 60:1-2).

And so the reality of this dawning of Yahweh's glory in his Son is rising and increasingly sensed, as is the night of darkness closing in on this world. We have already seen this with our Lord and those like him in Stephen, and as then, so now where the Spirit of life and peace shines in the darkness, even in the presence of a religious spirit. "You prepare a table before me in the presence of my enemies. You anoint my head with oil; my cup overflows" (Psalm 23:5).

The Light

In those days, when John the baptizer arose preceding the Lord and prepared the way for him and for the likes of Stephen, so the church rises up in the same spirit of Stephen and John. As Zechariah, John's father, prophesied about his son, so the Spirit of the Lord declares to his sons and daughters with a corporate calling as one child and as a prophetic church.

> And you, my child, will be called a prophet of the Most
> High; for you will go on before the Lord to prepare
> the way for him, to give his people the knowledge of
> salvation through the forgiveness of their sins, because
> of the tender mercy of our God, by which the rising sun
> will come to us from heaven to shine on those living in
> darkness and in the shadow of death, to guide our feet
> into the path of peace. (Luke 1:76-79)

In the face of the storm front coming upon the church to shaken it, awaken it, open its eyes, and remove all that is out of sync with the source of the light of this new day, peace will accompany these sons and daughters of the kingdom. His peace they will impart! That peace is the peace that Jesus gives, just as he said, "Peace I leave with you; my peace I give to you. I do not give to you as the world gives. Do not let your hearts be troubled and do not be afraid" (John 14:27).

While those living in such thick darkness are duped by the craftiness of Satan to see the darkness as something other than what it really is, the real light will be seen—even in the church! In the mercy and goodness of the Lord, there will be those spared—and not a few—who will see the glory of the Lord and take notice of their desperately needed Savior and Lord. "The people living in darkness have seen a great light; on those living in the land of the shadow of death a light has dawned" (Matthew 4:16).

Though a shadow of death has been over the church and in church in a way that was never intended, a light is dawning, and a new day rises on it. Outside the camp of death, restriction, and a lack of grace, the light, the truth, and the way will govern. "For God, who said, 'Let light shine out of darkness,' made his light to shine in our hearts to give us the light of the knowledge of God's glory displayed in the face of Christ" (2 Corinthians 4:6).

Chapter 6

Christchurch

An atmospheric and seismic shift is occurring! "Therefore we will not fear, though the earth give way … and the mountains quake with their surging" (Psalm 46:1-3). The Lord seeks to and will get our attention on what it is for us to know, hear, and listen to the voice of his Spirit. He speaks, even when he does not. He speaks one way or another. He is to be heard as we go on our way and often enough also by our stopping, pausing, and heeding. "Be still, and know that I am God" (Psalm 46:11).

This is the value of our sleep! That place of rest is where the Lord will speak through dreams. The Scriptures make that more than clear. The Lord still speaks through his Word and in keeping with his Word even today, including at the outset of every day. Note who sets the alarm! "He wakens me morning by morning, wakens my ear to listen like one being instructed" (Isaiah 50:4).

The Lord's voice, the voice of the Holy Spirit, is distinct from every other voice. Truly hearing and knowing his voice is imperative. This is the hour in which, as the church is being shaken, the church will learn and know how to distinguish his voice in a way that we have always been intended to know our Shepherd—by discerning his voice. "My sheep listen to my voice; I know them, and they follow me" (John 10:27).

Everything shakes when the Lord speaks! Those who have built their lives and churches on the foundation of the kingdom of God and humility of the King will not be shaken. Most assuredly, when the Lord speaks to his church, everything that can be shaken—that is not founded on the kingdom—will be shaken. Whenever he speaks, his voice shakes! "At that time his voice shook the earth, but now he has promised, 'Once more I will shake not only the earth but also the heavens'" (Hebrews 12:26, quoting Haggai 2:6). Take note that both the earth and the atmosphere (the heavens, naturally and spiritually) are shaken!

Relentless Shaking

It is not incidental that of all the cities (and regions) in the world, Christchurch (Canterbury), New Zealand should undergo such unusual, unique, and relentless shaking. The prophetic parallel is this: Christ's church is being shaken, and everything that can be shaken will be shaken.

As a family, we arrived in Auckland on the North Island of New Zealand on the same day, September 4, 2010, on which at 4:35 a.m., a magnitude 7.1 earthquake, known as the Canterbury (or Christchurch) Earthquake, struck forty kilometers (twenty-four miles) west of Christchurch on the South Island.

Incredibly and mercifully, with a population of 386,000, to my knowledge, no deaths occurred (that could be directly attributed to the quake). Injuries were also few for such an event. The quake on that day became the catalyst for ongoing, unnerving rumblings.

Then within six months, on February 22, 2011, at 12:51 p.m., a 6.3 magnitude quake struck, centered very close to Christchurch. In little over three hours, four more quakes at no less than magnitude 5 struck. Consequently, 185 people lost their lives, with many more injured.

The earthquakes on that day caused widespread damage across Christchurch, especially in the central city and eastern suburbs, with those suburbs significantly impacted by soil liquefaction (water pressure in the soil saturating and weakening its stability). Damage was exacerbated by buildings and infrastructure already weakened by the September 4, 2010 earthquake and its constant aftershocks.

Over half of the deaths occurred in the six-story Canterbury Television (CTV) Building, which collapsed and caught fire in the quake. While the damage was not limited to Christchurch only, significant landmarks, buildings, and infrastructure in Christchurch itself were impacted. Among these, notably, were structurally destroyed historic churches.

This unprecedented shaking on such a scale is remarkable to say the least in that up until August 7, 2012, more than eleven thousand aftershocks of magnitude 2 or more have been recorded, including twenty-six over 5.0 magnitude and two over 6.0 magnitude. The shaking continues.

On May 17, 2013, a magnitude 4.2 earthquake struck at 3:59 p.m. at a depth of seven kilometers (four miles) twenty-five kilometers (fifteen miles) southwest of Christchurch. Gladly and mercifully, there were no reports (that I came across) of injuries.

Revealing Our Hearts

Such an event as this is made all the more sobering when, as with life-changing things, it is brought very close to home. While we were not anywhere near the quake on the day we landed in Auckland, the sense of the impact of this shaking was in the air among those whose nation this was. The same is true when in our churches, among our churches in our neck of the woods, or in the churches across the board, sobering and revealing birth pains of a new day for the church are at hand.

Our hearts are being revealed with this shaking of Christ's church. As the Lord's people, we must see why we should be disturbed and troubled by things being out of our control. Those who know their Lord and grow in grace know that he is good and that all is well, even when everything else cries out otherwise.

> I sought the LORD, and he answered me; he delivered me from all my fears. Those who look to him are radiant; their faces are never covered with shame. This poor man called, and the LORD heard him; he saved him out of all his troubles. The angel of the LORD encamps around those who fear him, and he delivers them. (Psalm 34:4-7)

Kingdom's Call

We could not have envisaged the prophetic magnitude of this visit with our friends Mal and Shi in New Zealand when we first connected with them nine months previous in January 2010. The threads of the Lord's tapestry are not often clear (at first, at least) in life, at school, in college, at work, at church, in this world, etc.

At best, we see things "in part" (1 Corinthians 13:9). What may well look ordinary or messy from the underside (backend) of the tapestry of life in this world and with church nevertheless is a work of grace and art. That is the way in which, as with a work in progress, the Creator and builder is also on the job. "For we are God's handiwork, created in Christ Jesus" (Ephesians 2:10).

Preceding our arrival in New Zealand to meet our friends, on the day when the initial seismic trigger went off in Christchurch, we first met Mal and Shi face-to-face in June 2010. It was at Kingdom's Call, a gathering of the Lord's people from across the church in Tasmania and beyond with the summons from the Spirit for the church to "Arise, Shine" (Isaiah 60:1-3).

I had not experienced till that time such a profound measure and sense of rest and peace in the way it accompanied my overseeing of that gathering. This was starkly contrasted by the way in which a few days prior, the loathing and hostility of the religious spirit attacked. You can be sure that when the light of the day dawns and God's people arise, even as everything that can be shaken begins to be shaken, darkness is troubled, disturbed, and furious.

The threads that God used to bring this remarkable time together (Kingdom's Call), like so much of what he does, reinforced how awesome he is and his ways are. Our God is extraordinary in his engineering, orchestration, and tapestry of life and purpose. His sovereignty over all as Creator and Lord is indescribable, "for all things serve you" (Psalm 119:91).

Timing

Time serves him, for he is Lord over it. Time submits to him! Even as he is Lord of time—we who are in him and he in us—so time submits to those in step with the Spirit. Without anxiety ruling our steps, with the Lord being our peace and "though I walk in the midst of trouble" (Psalm 138:7), the timing of everything comes together. His is the hand on the clock! As the old song goes, "He's got the whole world in his hand!"

Truly, "There is a time for everything" (Ecclesiastes 3:1-8), and "The end of a matter is better than its beginning, and patience is better than pride. Do not be quickly provoked in your spirit, for anger resides in the lap of fools" (Ecclesiastes 7:8-9). "The wise heart will know the proper time and procedure. For there is a proper time and procedure for every matter" (Ecclesiastes 8:5-6), and "calmness can lay great offenses to rest" (Ecclesiastes 10:4).

Listen to Him!

Knowing the Lord, knowing his timing, knowing his voice, and listening to him must be the highest priority of the church. This is the mountain of the Lord! This is where the Father's voice is heard and the revelation of Jesus' glory is made known. It is there we are taken, prophetically speaking, where the distinction between our flesh, a religious spirit, and the like are sifted. There we are both humbled and lifted up!

When Jesus was transfigured before Peter, James, and John on the mountain, in that high place, one of the most important and valuable (few) words were spoken to them by God our Father. This Word of God was spoken in the context of his followers being in a good place. They were with the Lord. They were in his presence. Amazing things were happening. Yet in that good place, they made their best effort in their own strength, out of fear, to accommodate Jesus.

Truly, the focus is the Son! But seeing what was necessary and doing what was required were redefined for them. The landscape is the Way, and he must have supremacy over and above our way. We will know who he is as Lord, and hear what he says as gospel—the good news—for "the LORD is good" (Nahum 1:7). By the Word of God, the Father speaks! "This is my Son, whom I love; with him I am well pleased. Listen to him!" (Matthew 17:5, Mark 9:7)

When God speaks, Christ's church shakes! It is a good shaking! "When the disciples heard this, they fell facedown to the ground, terrified. But Jesus came and touched them. 'Get up,' He said. 'Don't be afraid'" (Matthew 17:6-7). As Christ's church shakes, its Lord reassures it. He comes up close and personal. He touches his people. He speaks to them as he lifts his church up from where it has been brought low, imparting the power of the truth that "There is no fear in love. But perfect loves drives out fear" (1 John 4:18).

The end result and purpose of this shaking love are so that we will lift up our eyes and hearts to the one our eyes are to be fixed on first and foremost. Listen to him! "When they looked up, they saw no one accept Jesus" (Matthew 17:8).

That which was built (and is being dismantled) was either built for a time or built as a sign to point to a greater reality. The shadow of the former things lengthens as the day sets on one age, even while the day dawns on the "powers of the coming age" (Hebrews 6:5).

> As Jesus was leaving the temple, one of his disciples said to him, "Look, Teacher! What massive stones! What magnificent buildings!" "Do you see all these great buildings?" replied Jesus. "Not one stone here will be left on another; everyone will be thrown down" … "What I say to you, I say to everyone: 'Watch!'" (Mark 13:1-2, 37)

Listen to him! Watch! The living stone (cornerstone) by which all is accurately measured and truly subject builds with his living stones, raising up a spiritual house.

> As you come to him, the Living stone—rejected by humans but chosen by God and precious to him—you also, like living stones, are being built into a spiritual house to be a holy priesthood, offering spiritual sacrifices acceptable to God through Jesus Christ.

For in Scripture it says, "See, I lay a stone in Zion, a chosen and precious cornerstone, and the one who trusts in him will never be put to shame."

Now to you who believe, this stone is precious. But to those who do not believe, "The stone the builders rejected has become the cornerstone," and, "A stone that causes people to stumble and a rock that makes them fall." (1 Peter 2:6-8)

"See to it that you do not refuse him who speaks" (Hebrews 12:25).

Chapter 7

Replacing the Lens

Revival and awakening are at hand! The Holy Spirit engineers and orchestrates this. One of the outstanding features will be that Jesus' lordship and sovereignty will be known in and through the church. It will be as though we really do believe in Immanuel (God with us) and that Jesus is Lord of our lives and over all things.

The reason for what may well be seen as a new reformation of the church will be because the church will no longer see the kingdom of God through the lens of church, but rather, the church will see itself through the lens of its Lord and his kingdom. The new lens will be "Seek first his kingdom and his righteousness" (Matthew 6:33).

Church will not remain looking only as we have become accustomed to seeing it. The dramatic change there will be is the result of a dramatic shift in focus. Without the impediments of days past, with our sin-based lens, a grace-based lens will have us see ourselves and others very differently. "So from now on we regard no one from a worldly point of view" (2 Corinthians 5:16), or after the flesh.

A profound change in the way in which we understand what it is to be the church and the way in which we do church will occur because of the way in which we will see the Lord himself as he is. We will, as the church, represent the kingdom of God in a way not only as well as, but also far better than we have before.

The Lord displaces and replaces the lens through which we see him and his kingdom. We have long looked upon the Lord and the Scriptures through the lens of church as we have grown up knowing or come into it as it is. Believing that what we are familiar with is the church and church is distorted when the lenses are back to front, for we see the Lord and his kingdom through our church lens.

The Lord is much, much greater, more personal, more creative, more at home, more forgiving, more secure, more understanding, more gracious, and more of much that could be said than what we generally portray both in church and as the church.

Notwithstanding, what we have and do reflect his goodness to date. What we have revealed of his love and nature has got us here by his grace and is to be saluted and applauded. This is especially so when we have revealed the Lord in such a hostile environment as this world for so long as well as contending with the religious spirit opposing the Lord's people from within. "For it is commendable if someone bears up under the pain of unjust suffering because they are conscious of God" (1 Peter 2:19).

While this is true and truly noble, we still must see ourselves as we really are as it stands. The battle for the Lord's supremacy as the way things really are and in the way we live as though this is true will take a move of the Spirit that we have not known of this magnitude for a shift in our focus and posture to take place. The Holy Spirit will move among us in such a way so as to undo what the Lord never did, to see the way we do as we do, which is not of him, or at best, a distant place between where he is and where we are.

Adjusting the Lens

A way to describe this is much like when we look through binoculars the opposite way from their intended use. What we see in turning them around is at a much greater distance than the ability that the binoculars have. When the right way around we see more clearly what is otherwise distant. The binoculars are being turned around back to their intended use!

The kingdom lens draws us close to God! Through it we see more clearly that Jesus has taken away all that would separate us from our heavenly Father. A religious spirit, on the other hand, with the binoculars (the lenses) back to front, creates a vast distance between us, the members of his body, and God in a way that is contrary to the grace and truth that is in Jesus. "But if we walk in the light as he is in the light, we have fellowship with one another, and the blood of Jesus, his Son, purifies us from all sin" (1 John 1:7).

When the church sees the way it is intended to by the light and through the eyes of the Lord, then the view is very different and truly wonderful. This can be an extremely difficult hurdle to overcome to receive this if we have been so adjusted to things the way they have been, being the other way around, as being the way we have believed they are meant to be.

When we adapt to the lack of light around us and walk more in darkness than light, we reason that this is how life is and that this is church. Though we may be unaware of it, the adjustment we make to the light that we have causes us to settle with believing that this is what it is like to know Jesus.

For "the people of the light" (Luke 16:18), it is the extent to which they see and receive the light himself that determines and exposes the amount of darkness they do or don't walk in, just as the level of light in the natural is what determines the measure of darkness there is.

Eyes to See

What we see with and how we see are crucial!

> The eye is the lamp of the body. If your eyes are healthy, your whole body will be full of light. But if your eyes are unhealthy, your whole body will be full of darkness. If then the light within you is darkness, how great is that darkness! (Matthew 6:22-23)

The changing lens at hand will have us say, with healthy, clear, and seeing eyes (spiritually), no matter what is against us, that greater still than the darkness is that God is for us. Seeing the light as he is causes us to rise up, time after time, to say it as Paul said it,

> And we know that in all things God works for the good of those who love him, who have been called according to his purpose …

Who shall separate us from the love of Christ? Shall trouble or hardship or persecution or famine or nakedness or danger of sword? ... No, in all these things we are more than conquerors through him who loved us.

For I am convinced that neither death nor life, neither angels nor demons, neither the present nor the future, nor any powers, neither height nor depth, nor anything else in all creation, will be able to separate us from the love of God that is in Christ Jesus our Lord. (Romans 8:28, 35, 37-39)

Unbelief and darkness dissipate where the light and truth we have in Jesus shine! Where the incorrect lens through which we have seen the Lord diminishes the reality of the goodness and power of God in Christ, then it's time for new eyes to see the light himself and hear again, "I am the way and the truth and the life" (John 14:6).

The Way

The boldness of heaven is coming upon the church and in our activities as the church, as was evident in the days of Acts. The Spirit will produce this with an assurance and confidence we have lacked. He will marshal this courage consistent with the gentleness, grace, truth, and power of our Lord Jesus.

In order to get where he leads us, the King and his kingdom will overshadow the church (with his light and glory, which are greater than darkness) by means that he chooses, even should these means prove profoundly uncomfortable and exposing.

The only discomfort we are really in for is the distinction between where we are and what has been of the flesh—as distinct from how things really are in God's kingdom, when earthed, as Jesus demonstrated. Greater light and understanding is before us with what it means when the Lord says, "Not by might nor by power, but by my Spirit" (Zechariah 4:6).

The church will, in the Lord's love for it, be humbled by the Lord and his light in order to rise, shine, and boldly declare that Jesus is Lord without fear, without shame, and completely secure as the eyes of his body focus on "him who called you out of darkness into his wonderful light" (1 Peter 2:9). With the Spirit as our most treasured companion, revealing the light himself to us, then the love, greatness, and goodness of God will be proclaimed.

A corporate echo of Paul's declaration to the Romans will be heard throughout the church walking in the light in days to come for the church that is at home and secure in God's great love. With a Spirit-empowered boldness like that on the day of Pentecost, these friends, family, and soldiers of the Way will be heard proclaiming, "For I am not ashamed of the gospel, because it is the power of God that brings salvation to everyone who believes" (Romans 1:16).

Moreover, these sons and daughters (both natural and spiritual) will prophesy. Young men will see visions. Old men will dream dreams. Both men and women, by the Spirit, will prophesy. There will be wonders and signs. Many will call upon the name of the Lord and be saved (Acts 2:17-21). This is both at the door and already in the house.

The Lord's majesty, goodness, and power are in the air! The lens is changing, and the church is called to no longer be on the back foot. Recognizing what on earth is happening will become clearer to those who will discern the acts of the Holy Spirit in our day, just as the early church did in its times.

Again, to reinforce the message of the times in which we have entered as the church, understand this: the winds of the Holy Spirit are at hand, and the landscape of church as we think of it is moving toward unprecedented change in our lives personally and as the church corporately. God is replacing the lens! Resistance to this life-giving renewal and restoration of the church is foolishness and a sign of immaturity.

The Wisdom of Gamaliel

It is time for the wisdom of Gamaliel (of Acts 5:33-40) to return! Let Gamaliel's wisdom be seen among the leaders, elders, fathers, mothers, and parents of the previous move of God, which sought to establish freedom from the very restrictions it has itself been imposing. Let their humility, wisdom, and virtue come to the forefront.

In the face of any sense of uncertainty about what on earth is going on with the church yet with confidence in the power of grace over all things, let them be heard declaring among themselves and publicly,

> In the present case I advise you: Leave these men alone! Let them go! For if their purpose or activity is of human origin, it will fail. But if it is from God, you will not be able to stop these men; you will only find yourselves fighting against God. (Acts 5:38-39)

The Holy Spirit awakens his people to the distinction in spirit, between death and life, flesh and Spirit, being without love, as Jesus loves, and truly having his love. This will become increasingly clear as the glory of the Lord rises upon his people.

The grace of the day at hand will magnify our strength (or lack of it) in our relationships. The lens through which we see unity, when corrected, will enable us to see that Jesus has already established it by his blood shed on the cross. This will reshape what we have done in seeking to create unity without ever truly achieving it.

The church is more than structures, programs, and administration. Such as these and the like are not the Way but rather are assigned to serve the Way. The way of the church is a person, and he is a great King with a glorious kingdom that he is earthing through the church in relationships (what I like to call power lines).

Disrupting Our Way

The Spirit will disrupt our ways in order to reveal that Jesus is the Way. There is no safer or more life-giving place than the Lord when he truly is Lord of his church. The renewal of this is by virtue of the Holy Spirit becoming the governing spirit in the church. "Now the Lord is the Spirit, and where the Spirit of the Lord is, there is freedom" (2 Corinthians 3:17).

In a Sunday morning service that I attended during 2012, I witnessed the Lord, in his love for his church and in his intention to enlarge its heart, seeking to relax God's people and alter the order of service during worship to convey something significant and prophetically insightful.

He did this by overruling everything going smoothly when the projector for the words on the front screen failed. The back screen for the worship team was, however, working. All that was needed was for church to turn 180 degrees. It was as simple as that!

The people of the church failed though to recognize simplicity and the prophetic turning around required. Tradition and structure could neither see this nor yield to being at home in the Lord's ways being different to ours. When we are comfortable and at home with the Lord, we are able to make whatever adjustments are necessary. The church will be led in these days and the days to come by those who know and are sensitive to the ways of the Spirit.

What this looks like is where we are going, and it's as safe and secure as the Lord himself. It may not be all clean and tidy in the way we would like it to be. Our Father, though, as a family man, reproduces the humility of his Son in us while lovingly evicting the pride that has kept us from truly knowing him.

In love for his church and for those yet to enter in, the Lord has been gently shaking his church for some time now. Blessed are those who have recognized him in this. The gentle seismic shaking has been a forewarning of the much greater shaking before us. The shaking is necessary and good in order for us to become, sooner rather than later, the salt of the earth and light of a world that so deeply needs to see Jesus.

Separation

A spiritual separation is occurring across the church. This shaking and sifting is a valley of decision in which a choice must be made as to whom or what is truly our Lord. Somewhere along the way, for whatever reason may be given, the main thing—the Lord himself, our primary compass bearing and focus—was robbed.

Those God has, is, and will yet draw to himself as believers and part of the church should know no hypocrisy between their faith and church.

The church, if anything, is to be an authentic witness of God's saving grace and approachableness in reality. What Jesus died for and saved us out of should be clearly evident in "life and doctrine" (1 Timothy 4:16).

The very foundation of faith is being tested! God does this in order to see where our hearts and loyalties lie. Is what we say we believe really how things are? As Jesus said, "No one can serve two masters" (Matthew 6:24).

Simply put to yet again reinforce what has been said: what it means to have the lens replaced and be with Jesus outside the camp is about our hearts looking to and being one in spirit with our Savior and Lord, Jesus—trusting in his sacrifice and remaining in his love (John 15:1-17). This gateway to salvation and growing in grace is humility!

Pride and fear is the camp we are called out from. That camp is where the flesh rules and we are sin-focused. In that camp, we see life through the lens of what we must do in order to be right in God's sight and the sights of others. That camp depends on works, is based on pride and fear, and is not on Christ's finished work on the cross (though it may appear and say otherwise).

That camp masquerades, "having a form of godliness but denying its power" (2 Timothy 3:5). It relies on self-righteousness, human-made traditions, and religious structures. It is imprisoning and imposes limits upon the grace and freedom there are in Christ.

As I also have said previously, what it means to be outside the camp is about our hearts looking to and being one in spirit with our Savior and Lord, Jesus—trusting in his sacrifice and remaining in his love. "Let us, then, go to him outside the camp, bearing the disgrace that he bore" (Hebrews 13:13).

Truly, the gateway to salvation and growing in grace is humility! The foundation upon which we come to Christ in the first place and always after never changes. We come to the Lord in humility and live our lives before him and one another on that basis. In this way, we are like Jesus: "he humbled himself" (Philippians 2:8). The Scripture is clear on what the church must embody and be a witness to. "This is how we know we are in him: Whoever claims to live in him must live as Jesus did" (1 John 2:5-6).

Chapter 8

The Glory of the Lord

As surely as the dawning of a day in the natural precedes the source of its light, so the glory of the Lord rises on his church preceding Jesus' return. When dawn progressively breaks, what was not clear beforehand becomes increasingly visible and understood.

At the risk of over-repeating it, I'll broadcast the kingdom's call again. Heralded by the Holy Spirit, particularly over recent years, the summons has gone out and continues to go forth for the church to

> arise, shine, for your light has come, and the glory of the LORD rises upon you. See, darkness covers the earth and thick darkness is over the peoples, but the LORD rises upon you and his glory appears over you. Nations will come to your light, and kings to the brightness of your dawn. (Isaiah 60:1-3)

The light of God's glory in Christ is both dawning and breaking through the veil that has limited seeing well. The way things really are is being revealed with greater sharpness. The disclosure of what has been under the cloak of the cover of darkness is coming to light. Clearer distinctions between light and darkness, truth and falsehood, and righteousness and unrighteousness are emerging.

The Vision

While sitting alone in the lounge room of our home one evening in May 2000 in Barrington, Tasmania, in the months after Tina Maree and I had been married, I looked out the window in the direction of Mount Roland. Suddenly, but peacefully and invigoratingly, an unannounced, open-eyed vision was given to me, bringing the above passage of Scripture to life.

In the vision, as I stood out in the open, I looked heavenward. Spread out across the entire sky from north to south and east to west, there was a thick canopy—a veil and shroud—over the whole earth. There was barely any light, because heaven and earth were separated by the thick darkness covering the earth.

With my right hand raised in intercession, I called on the Lord, saying, "Come, Lord! Come!" I interceded with that sense when "deep calls to deep" (Psalm 42:7) in the spirit of the church's inspired final prayer, "The Spirit and the bride say, 'Come!'" (Revelation 22:17)

I repeated this call three times. Then with an assuring sense of rest and peace, the Spirit of God conveyed that I had been heard and to be still and wait. I was aware that this patience was important and had purpose. The time that passed in quietness was, paradoxically, long and short. I could not measure it!

Then that same compulsion to intercede rose up once more. As beforehand, this intercession was initiated by heaven and earthed through my response. My heart was awakened as I did this, opening my eyes to see how God's house is truly called "a house of prayer for all nations" (Isaiah 56:7). With an even greater confidence and sense of authority in the intercession this time, I vocalized the end-time prayer just a few more times.

Then, wonderfully, above and before me and a bit to my right, the thick darkness was pierced. The light of the Lord's glory shone brilliantly as it broke through. It did this just as the sun streams forward with its shafts of light through clouds to the earth, displaying radiant silver linings that are as hems on the clouds' edges.

From what was like a small and progressive opening up to a large and then rapidly increasing break in a dam wall, I found myself witnessing an outpouring of the floodgates of heaven. The glory of the Lord was magnificent! This was very reassuring!

The faith needed in the darkness up until this point had required great courage. The Lord made clear what had not been near as clear as it was becoming. The shroud between heaven and earth simply yielded to the power above it.

As the erosion of this bleak veil increased, I was captivated. The darkness rapidly dissipated. Innumerous angels began advancing through the portal toward the earth, each clearly assigned to an appointed place to which they darted.

The activity of the angels, their devotion to and love for the Lord, and their relationship in connectedness of heart with the Lord's purposes and the church were amazing. The Word of the Lord was magnified even more than I was already aware as I saw their ministry and authority in this context. Yes, truly, the church will know that "Are not all angels ministering spirits sent to serve those who will inherit salvation?" (Hebrews 1:14)

Hidden up until now under the dark shadow of the once immense enveloping cloud, demonic hordes began to be seen and were repulsed at the exposure they received. These deceiving and contorted creatures were in total disarray and in a highly chaotic state, going this way and that, seeking to hide from the dawning light of the Righteous One (Isaiah 24:16). The reality of Scripture came triumphantly to the fore. "He reveals the deep and hidden things; he knows what lies in darkness, and light dwells with him" (Daniel 2:22).

Then, hurled and cast down out of the cloud as though under my feet, as feet representative of the Lord's body, fell "The great dragon ... that ancient serpent called the devil, or Satan, who leads the whole world astray ... They triumphed over him" (Revelation 12:9, 11).

At this, I saw a very large angel descend from the glory above. In its hand was a victory torch much like an Olympic torch with its flame. Many trumpets sounded! Then I heard a voice saying, "Now have come the salvation and the power and the kingdom of our God, and the authority of his Messiah" (Revelation 12:10).

I stood at my post and watched these things in astonishment. I then saw the thick cloud of darkness receding slowly and being pushed back.

And as dark, brewing storm clouds in the natural gather their fierce intensity under opposing pressures in the atmosphere, this canopy of evil that had once permeated the air rolled back toward the horizon. It retreated in the direction before me, away from where the glory of the Lord increased overhead.

Incomprehensibly, as dense as the thick darkness over the earth had been prior to the Lord's coming in this way, as it rolled back, it became much greater in intensity. The atmosphere of its ink black and dreaded darkness was that of an enraged opponent who knew his hold was tenuous and unsustainable and that his time was short.

As I continued watching these profound and striking contrasts before me, between the glory and power of the Lord, as distinct from the hostility and enmity of the gross and foul darkness, something incredible and wonderful occurred.

Peter, a young man whom I knew in my youth who came to the Lord and then later turned away, was in the shadows of the gloomy darkness. I said to him, "Come home! Come home!" I watched in amazement at his deliverance as he came up out of that intensifying dark storm.

This prodigal son, having seen the glory and light of his Savior like never before, courageously set his heart on his one and only refuge and hope and returned to the safety of his true home in the light.

He walked up past and behind me, and as he did, the look of assurance on his face was something I will never forget. I sensed that he was representative of many such prodigals and the lost who will turn to the light, even as darkness increases.

Suddenly, and also extremely encouraging, a great army (in number and resolve) marched up in perfect order from behind me. These pressed forward into the fray of the dreaded darkness. Without a doubt among these fearless and well-equipped soldiers were Peter and other captives of the Lord. With this scene before me, I heard, "There will be no more delay!" (Revelation 10:6) With this, the vision ended!

Nations, kings, and leaders will be drawn to the light of the glory of Jesus both coming upon the world and in the flesh in God's people— the Lord's body—preceding his return. The testimony of Jesus will be powerfully evident in the humble and fearless like David, as those I saw march forth. They will be as a corporate David—"a man after my own heart; he will do everything I want him to do" (Acts 13:22).

In these days of shaking, while people become more fearful in their apprehension and having no comprehension of what is coming on the world, all those aligned with the kingdom of God will stand unshaken and lift up their heads. It's time to arise and shine as salt and light in the Spirit and strength of the Lord. Take courage!

> For God, who said, "Let light shine out of darkness," made his light shine in our hearts to give us the light of the knowledge of God's glory displayed in the face of Christ. But we have this treasure in jars of clay to show that this all-surpassing power is from God and not from us. We are hard pressed on every side, but not crushed; perplexed, but not in despair; persecuted, but not abandoned; struck down, but not destroyed. We always carry around in our body the death of Jesus, so that the life of Jesus may also be revealed in our body. (2 Corinthians 4:6-9)

The faith that was needed in the darkness till now and the truly great faith that was required—and the faith that will yet be called forth—forged and forges love, insight, and courage. It is more than proportionate to the fury of Satan who knows by seeing such Christ-like love, faith, and fearlessness that his time is indeed short.

On the other hand, those allied to Satan find that the darkness effectually becomes thicker around them. Their blindness increases. They cannot see it, and we may wonder why when it seems so very evident to us what on earth is going on. But we see what we do because we are, by grace, not where they are—where we too once were.

Our intercession for them and God's love in us toward them will be as others have shown us in order that we would see. The light and power of Jesus alone can save these out of such peril, just as they (his light and power) have delivered us. The testimony of Jesus in what he has done for us has the power to do the same for them. Let what God has done for you be told!

Praise and Worship

Our love for the Lord and the humility in which we walk before him at the expense of fear go as deep as closeness and oneness with the Lord can possibly go on this earth. Those who are already born again, those returning to their true home, and those coming into the kingdom all share the riches of God's mercy and grace. They rise together as one as an army and family to love, praise, and serve the worthy One.

The worship that we have known, wonderful as it has been, is going to go to much greater levels. We have tasted it; yet it has been but a deposit of a place in the Spirit and the sound coming. Praise will increase, and its glory is immeasurable!

This praise of angels and every creature comes to an everlasting crescendo, spontaneously and freely, with (welcome) loud singing, declaring,

> Worthy is the Lamb, who was slain, to receive power and wealth and wisdom and strength and honor and glory and praise! ... To him who sits on the throne and to the Lamb be praise and honor and glory and power, for ever and ever!" (Revelation 5:12-13)

Love for Jesus

There is great richness of love for the Father and the Son already here; yet it is coming in greater measure. The love of God for us in his Son and our love for them will be seen and understood in no less a remarkable way than they were in the early church. The power of what this looks like will be by the display of humility, so distinctly contrasted with pride, and for what they each produce.

Luke's account (Luke 7:36-50) of the woman whose life was turned around because of Jesus' love to awaken those who saw her otherwise (as a sinner) was so that they would see what God sees and know how deeply God loves. This too will be seen—as then, so now—to revive what has been lost of the glory of our salvation (intimacy of relationship with God) for each and every one of us.

Who will love him more? Those who know and remember how powerful is God's love in his Son, in the reality of what life has been like, in both the good and foolish choices we've made. These humble and contrite who walk in amazing grace, as fresh today as they knew it at first, are a sign to the church that it has lost what God has found.

What is precious to God in the extent to which he would go to show his love for sinners, he will display in the times during which we have entered as he did at the time during which his love in his Son was manifested so wonderfully and personally on this earth. Once again, the Lord is coming in the flesh—in his body, in his members—before his return to reveal the very One coming in all his glory.

The glory of the Lord will be seen, even as thick darkness covers the earth. While the thick darkness both recedes and intensifies, the activity of heaven will be clear and manifest. What the early church has experienced (as well as others throughout Scripture) of the love of God and the glory of the Lord will now be revealed to us for Jesus' name's sake.

Chapter 9

A Jealous God

Love—nothing surpasses it! In all of creation with all that is great, wonderful, glorious, remarkable, spectacular, and awesome, love is behind, in, and surpasses it. In all that is life and good, it stems from the truth that "God is love" (1 John 4:16).

God's love for us in his Son, and that same love in us, has supremacy over all things. To know this love truly is to know God. And to have his love truly is to love as he loves. "Whoever lives in love lives in God, and God in them" (1 John 4:16).

God's love never fails! His love never quits! He stills loves the world, and this will not change at any stage. "Jesus Christ is the same yesterday and today and forever" (Hebrews 13:8). In God's love for the world, he is jealous for our love for him and that our love for him is above our love for all else. When loving him takes supremacy, we love all else as it is to be loved—with his love.

All that unfolds and comes to pass in these last days is so that the world will know that it cannot live without relationship—closeness and oneness—with its maker, sustainer, deliverer, and life. Neither can the church, the Lord's people, of all people. We are called to reveal him who says, "you whom I have upheld since your birth, and have carried since you were born. Even to you old age and gray hairs I am he, I am he who will sustain you. I have made you and I will carry you; I will sustain you and I will rescue you" (Isaiah 46:3-4).

In his love for his people and the world, God is jealous. He is jealous for our lives, our love, and our freedom. He is jealous that there would be nothing between us and him or one another. "Do not worship any other god, for the LORD, whose name is Jealous, is a jealous God" (Exodus 34:14).

A Snapshot

Here then is a snapshot of the Lord's jealousy for his people—a people who declared their love for him and a people whose love was tested! I was among them. I grew up among such as these, through whom my faith was grounded, nurtured, and nourished. I love them! These are my brothers and sisters in the grace of our Lord Jesus.

The general context of this story may sound familiar. You may well identify with this snapshot in a church that you are a part of, or have been part of, or know.

Something was not working. Something wasn't right. Something had to be fixed. A time for a change had come! It's just that the change that came was not the change these believers sought in the way it came.

At first, the willingness to change was there. This was personally and publicly expressed with a desire to surrender to the Spirit to have his way, whatever that meant. It was encouraging to watch then when on a particular occasion in the months following, there was clear evidence of the Holy Spirit moving on the ground of this humility.

What this meant was not easy and at times painful for these believers to go against the culture and tradition with which they were so familiar. Not surprisingly, then, cracks began to form even at an early stage, with polarization occurring and a sifting of where people truly stood. Faith began to be seen to have two quite different faces.

The reticence in heart among a number of the people was seen in their holding back and questioning the direction. Among others, however, there remained a shared enthusiasm that something good was happening sufficient to risk moving forward in going somewhere other than where they had been, had so long known, and could not remain.

The evidence of the welcome change occurring for those who could receive it was especially seen when at times, in prayer prior to a Sunday morning together, the Lord's presence was such that staying put was all you wanted to do. Not only so, but it seemed like it would have been a good move if the gathering assembly in church came to where the

Lord was, where we met in prayer. This perhaps would have helped the church to see what the Lord had spoken so clearly to this particular church about—that "My house will be called a house of prayer" (Isaiah 56:7, Matthew 21:13, Mark 11:17, Luke 19:46).

But could we do it? It is telling to see the power of what tradition and what we are accustomed to dictate the Way himself. That sounds like pretty serious stuff when it is put like that—and it is! For we are being made to see this when we are bound—imprisoned, mastered—by doing things we have only ever known. That being the case, our faith is lacking, his grace corrupted, and our security has become something other than the Lord.

That we would do what we do and not what God is doing is a sign in itself that we have lost our bearings with knowing the Way as he would be known. With good reason and great purpose, therefore, Christ's church is shaken!

In love for us, he died that we would know him as much as and far better than anyone and anything, including much of what we have resigned ourselves to believing is how we are to function as church as we have known it. Our God is far greater than the fear we walk in by what we are bound to by our order of service.

Yes, this is sobering! But in his great love, the jealous One will not yield his glory to another. The Lord is awakening us to understand that either by his Spirit or by any other means, "People are slaves to whatever has mastered them" (2 Peter 2:19).

There were those who left. There were those who came. There were those who didn't know what to make of it. There was change, though—and encouraging change, at that, for those who knew that going back was not an option and that pressing past the pressure to go back would be worth it. So they kept moving forward, strengthened by the Spirit and eager to take risks while seeking to walk with everyone on deck as much as possible.

Then, like a hammer to glass, a decision was made. If I was able to articulate the sense of what I (and not I alone) encountered of the grieving of the Spirit, I would falter in conveying it well. You could sense that something so deep had shifted spiritually. This unfolded over time in a bittersweet way.

The worship would continue and at times to go somewhere that was beyond the known and expected—to a place and at a level that was, to describe it simply while inadequately, truly good. Yet at other times, it was a step (or two or three) back to where things were— somewhere before the heart cry that something was missing had been heard.

When there were steps in a forward direction, however, along with those in worship, we were encouraged. We responded to calls to pray and not just via the pastoral prayer. By gathering around, spontaneously or as a reflection of the way a family rallies in time of need, we would pray for the one(s) or situation(s) to be lifted up to the Lord in intercession there and then.

We would also pray for one another just where we were. We were up close and personal with each other, picturing what our Lord is like with us when we let him get close. This taste of being a house of prayer reflected, even if only in a small measure, what love, fellowship, and something truly living and powerful about church looks like.

And it was during this bittersweet period, with a decline in fervor for the change that most knew was needed, that what I wrote about in chapter seven happened. The Lord, in his love, clearly sought to get the church's attention in a prophetic and symbolic way. In his intention to enlarge the heart of this body of believers, he sought to relax our posture and redesign and re-landscape the order of service during worship.

The One who was jealous for his people's love more than our service and worship did this by overruling everything going smoothly when the projector for the words on the front screen failed. The back screen for the worship team, however, worked. All that was needed was for church to turn 180 degrees. That's where the Lord was. It was as simple as that!

But it never happened! The ease of doing it was hard! The difficulty for church to turn around (in repentance for where it was going) and toward the Lord was demonstrated both practically and prophetically that day. Tradition and structure could neither see this nor yield to being at home with the Way being different and coming in another form.

It was difficult and heart-wrenching to see how the Lord was not recognized in this and other ways. A falling away from grace occurred.

Our drawing back was evident in how we responded (or rather, did not respond).

An exposure of the church's true heart was being revealed. It emerged that only that which was of its own kind in practice and spirit could ultimately be received. This belied the grace being professed. As much as this is not easy to see—to say the least—this exposing of a part of the character of the religious spirit in this guise was, insightfully, a spirit of racism. Again, fear is at the root of how these attributes manifest.

We must know and understand that at any given time, we are—any one of us and all of us—either party to the Holy Spirit or not. This is a spiritual issue! "For our struggle is not against flesh and blood, but against the rulers, against the authorities, against the powers of this dark world and against the spiritual forces of evil in the heavenly realms" (Ephesians 6:12).

This turning away from grace, rooted more deeply than addressed on the ground during the course of those days, shifted the compass bearing of the church not only 180 degrees, but also into a no man's land. This decision and change of course ultimately resulted in the sealing of a limit to which those in this family were prepared to go—yet not before the Lord would make his thoughts known. The test of our absolute surrender to Jesus came to its climax!

At a crucial stage before this turnaround was set in concrete, it was decided by the members to stop for three weeks by waiting on the Lord. The intention to hear from him to see if he had something to say was exemplary. This was wisdom, this was family, and this was good—even at this eleventh hour!

There was always a heart in those holding out hope, in the knowledge of the need for change in the first place, to keep thinking the best of those who saw otherwise, especially now that a measure of that change had come. Such was the authenticity of the love, grace, and humility of their hearts.

This is not to say that these pioneers and risk-takers were perfect. No, they were not! Remember that "we have this treasure in jars of clay" (2 Corinthians 4:7). At the end of the day, we will not hear, "Well done, good and perfect servant!" Rather, we will hear, "Well done, good and faithful servant!" (Matthew 25:21, 23) Faithfulness to the Lord and one another is what earns one the salute of the Lord.

As a corporate family and body of the Lord's people, we fell well short of even how family in the natural would generally act. Simply talking with one another in love, with all our differences, has that stamp of life on it as family. Friends sit down over a meal or a coffee without the atmosphere that we tend to come under in church or with matters about church and in a meeting to resolve things.

A gathering as family and friends in that spirit, as happens in life outside of church, was sought. Appreciating what that meant was no doubt difficult if it had never truly been experienced as a part of church. That relationship of love, life, and trust never happened, though. Fear presided instead—paradoxically, where fear has no room among those who know their God.

Something changes that is commonly experienced when going to church. We come together in a way that is unnatural in life as we live it otherwise and in a way that is out of step with the Spirit. A disconnection can occur in our relationships in a church meeting in a way that is not usually there in most any other place. This is extraordinary when it is intended, in the way the Lord has designed us, for there to be power lines of life and relationship among us in the most invigorating, sharpening, strengthening, and encouraging way.

We were not made to blunt or darken each other, and when this happens, we can know assuredly that we are not in step with wisdom or the Spirit. For "As iron sharpens iron, so one person sharpens another" (Proverbs 27:17), and "If we claim to have fellowship with him and yet walk in the darkness, we lie and do not live out the truth. But if we walk in the light, as he is in the light, we have fellowship with one another, and the blood of Jesus, his Son, purifies us from all sin" (1 John 1:6-7).

Exasperated Children

For the body of the Lord to be the body, truly, the whole body must be discerned, received, seen, and heard. There is a generation that is passing that built a foundation that had mixture. They heard for themselves as young children and in turn carried a culture within the church that said, "Children should be seen and not heard." The damage that this brought upon the thinking and culture of the kingdom in the church is gladly being redeemed. The winds of redemption are at hand!

The impact of such a demoralizing spirit to quench the life of family in the natural and spiritual has led to a great impoverishment of the church (let alone in society generally). Many of the spiritual children of the church have either jumped ship completely or simply gone where they could better breathe.

There were those, however, who remained, either to embellish that spirit in themselves unwittingly or (gratefully) who have in the grace of God survived and grown against the odds. Yet for so many of these literal and spiritual children, their parents (for the most part) did not heed the Word himself, which said, "Fathers, do not exasperate your children" (Ephesians 6:4). The children needed and wanted to be heard.

These parents have been, for the most part, honored by these children, as parents should be. These parents certainly did nurture their children in good measure, heeding "bring them up in the training and instruction of the Lord" (Ephesians 6:4). Nevertheless, there were exasperated (even embittered) sons and daughters whose parents did not let these children be recognized as those through whom the Lord would prepare the way for him as a new generation. In his wisdom, the Lord has let this happen to sift, sort, and refine his church.

We must understand, though, that these parents were also products of their generations, in which their parents and teachers handed down something less than what the church, by grace, was given as the salt and light that the world itself so desperately needed.

The children of the church who have not been able to speak up and have not been recognized as an indispensable part of the revelation of the Lord or equal part of the body, even though they have come of age, will now find freedom to be seen and heard.

The infants and children, both natural and in the Lord, who have always been part of the church, or have since come on board or still yet to come, must be seen, heard, and honored. Remember the Lord's words: "'Truly I tell you, whatever you did for one of the least of these brothers and sisters of mine, you did for me.' ... 'whatever you did not do for one of the least of these, you did not do for me'" (Matthew 25:40, 45).

These least and born again also have the Spirit! If we are to hear the Spirit, we must see the Lord in them and hear from the Lord in them. Our wisdom, humility, and growth are to receive them as Jesus did, both young children in the natural and spiritual. We are wise to let the humility and ability of children teach and remind us that "the kingdom of heaven belongs to such as these" (Matthew 19:13).

The power of the gospel of the kingdom is in the natural and spiritual children. They have keys in the very real spiritual battles in which we are engaged. When they are kept silent, we are weaker for it, and this gives access to the enemy where we are summoned to be victorious. They are warriors in their praise, and they are to be seen and heard, for "Through the praise of children and infants you have established a stronghold against your enemies, to silence the foe and the avenger" (Psalm 8:2).

The gates and doors of the kingdom of heaven open up and are earthed in and through the church where the church receives the kingdom in the only way that we can, just as we did when we were born again. To the church, as much as to those who would yet enter the kingdom of God, the Lord still speaks, saying, "Truly I tell you, unless you change and become like little children, you will never enter the kingdom of heaven" (Matthew 18:3).

Idolatry in the Church

Whatever the Holy Spirit does, in the way the Spirit always and only ever reveals the Father and the Son, through whomever and by whatever means, we make way for the Lord himself. However, when the foundation of our love, faith, and trust in God is compromised, when we walk personally or corporately contrary to it, we can be sure that in God's great love for and faithfulness to us, he should make known that he is a jealous God.

We must see idolatry for what it is! When we place something else before the Lord after having given him all, we are back where we said we didn't want to be and couldn't be any longer. That place was fear and self-preservation. It is a great insult and most erroneous thing when our identity and security in Jesus are forsaken.

The Lord is jealous for what we have said that he could have after having given him our absolute surrender. What we give over wholly to the Lord that is then the Lord's—our lives and church—and then take them back is truly falling away from grace. "You have forsaken the love you had at first" (Revelation 2:4).

The true form, structure, and worship of the church are Spirit. The Way of the church is a person: Jesus! We are followers of the Lord of heaven and earth, not a system, structure, program, order of service, or anything other than what is of the Spirit.

We see this as Jesus revealed it when he spoke to the Samaritans, whom he loved, through the Samaritan woman, whose heart and life he knew by the Spirit. He saw her under bondage, not only in her life personally but along with her people corporately. They knew not their God as he would have them know him—personally, intimately, and not by means externally.

Knowledge knows truly, even as Jesus knew this thirsting woman's heart, warts and all, and loved her for who she and the Samaritans were at heart. These seekers of God, in seeking to truly know and worship him, discerned, recognized, and received God as he came—as the real deal. Knowing is a matter of spirit and heart.

As Jesus said to this dear and teachable woman and her people and as he speaks likewise to us through her and them,

> A time is coming and has now come when the true worshippers will worship the Father in the Spirit and in truth, for they are the kind of worshippers the Father seeks. God is Spirit and his worshippers must worship in the Spirit and in truth. (John 4:23-24)

These amazing people, when hearing the way about the truth and finding the life, exchanged their outward focus for an inward reality with a resulting outward and authentic expression. These are those whom Jesus taught us through in the parable of the Good Samaritan (Luke 10:25-37).

Jesus illustrated an outward demonstration coming from an inward reality about who is a true neighbor and what it is to truly love. Jesus revealed this in the context of what was otherwise a religious spirit—a spirit of fear and pride—steering clear and standing at a distance, aloof, from giving witness to what godliness and power are.

The distinction between a form and the reality is as clear as clear be for those who have eyes to see, ears to hear, and hearts to receive this wisdom that comes from humility. The point of the insightful and telling story of the Good Samaritan, as much as anything, is this: it reveals the heart of the Son of God himself as gracious, merciful, and abounding in love and how those who are "conformed to the image of his Son" (Romans 8:29) do likewise as a people of the Way. Church, this is what outside the camp looks like! This is what it is to go to Jesus and follow the Son where he is and in what he is like, where love, closeness, oneness, and unity are revealed "on earth as it is in heaven (Matthew 6:10)."

The distinction between this heart and spirit and that of a religious spirit—a spirit of death—is indeed and tellingly so life and death. Lifelessness is what marks the nature of those governed by a spirit other than the Spirit of Jesus. A religious spirit leaves you for dead; the Spirit of the Lord is life-giving.

Yes, "If we walk in the light as he is in the light we have fellowship with one another" (1 John 1:7). You can know assuredly that if our fellowship is not happening, a religious spirit is behind it and in the air, hostile to the truth that "As iron sharpens iron, so one person sharpens another" (Proverbs 27:17).

Again, Jesus is jealous for our love, not our traditions or immovable positions that let those idols live on while they kill those for whom Jesus died that they would live—"that they may have life, and have it to the full" (John 10:10).

For those who are part of the church, whose picture of church is embedded in nothing (or little) being changed with how things are, be warned! If you keep holding on so tenaciously to a spirit that says, "This is how it is, and this is how it's always been, and that's not going to change on my watch," then know that the old guard without a heart is truly on life support.

The Lord in his love for his body remains faithful even to those who will not change. "If we are faithless, he remains faithful, for he cannot deny himself" (2 Timothy 2:13). In great love and faithfulness, he remains beside the deathbed of the lifeless members of his body. He both grieves and honors their passing!

Jesus Is Lord

As the light and as Lord, Jesus exposes Pharisees in their darkness with their determination to justify themselves for being a cut above the rest as the standard of righteousness in what they do and in their reasoning as to why they should distance and separate themselves from others at the expense of the very Scripture they purport to represent.

With a restless and relentless urge inspired by a compulsion of suspicion in seeking to find a single justifiable reason for bringing another down, we see them coming together as a pack of wolves. Arrogantly, they chomp at the bit to justify their distancing of themselves from having fellowship with or loving others apart from their own kind. The test is on their side of the court, not his who is the Way and Lord.

> Hearing that Jesus had silenced the Sadducees, the Pharisees got together. One of them, an expert in the law, tested him with this question: "Teacher, which is the greatest commandment in the Law?" Jesus replied, "'Love the Lord your God with all your heart and with all your soul and with all your mind.' This is the first and greatest commandment. And the second is like it: 'Love your neighbor as yourself.' All the Law and the Prophets hang on these two commandments." (Matthew 22:34-40)

The way we are to take—the way of love—as the members of Christ's body must be in oneness with the Way himself as the head of the body and as Lord. All that we do must be in submission to and subject to the Lord Jesus. "Do you not know that your bodies are temples of the Holy Spirit, who is in you, whom you have received from God?

You are not your own; you were bought with a price. Therefore honor God with your bodies" (1 Corinthians 6:19-20). These bodies are ours personally, and these bodies are his churches—the people of God, as a company and fellowship of believers—corporately meeting in various churches and locations locally and across the earth.

Jesus is Lord of a body—"like living stones, are being built into a spiritual house" (1 Peter 25). He is not, and his members are not, a church structure. Everything must be under him—"the living Stone—rejected by humans but chosen by God and precious to him" (1 Peter 2:4).

So if we truly do what we do as led by the Spirit, then if he is not doing something, we should not assume we must in order to appear godly. That would be being ungodly with the appearance of being godly.

Everything is subject to the leading and lordship of the Holy Spirit. If there is anyone who the church should know, it should be the Holy Spirit. He is our Lord, leading us always and only to Jesus to bring glory to Jesus and honor to God our Father. We must seek first, above all else, his kingdom and righteousness (Matthew 6:33).

Waiting on God

We return to a snapshot of the Lord's jealousy for his people. When, then, the Lord speaks out in order to seek to get our attention, he will do so through whatever instrument and by whatever means. When at a crucial stage, before completely turning away was set in concrete from the direction we sailed as a church for want of the Lord to move, a wise decision was made. It was first decided by the membership to stop for three weeks by waiting on the Lord in order to hear from him and know his heart. This was a good move in the right direction!

The Lord was so eager to speak to the people he loved with a longing that they grow in grace that on the very next evening after that decision and while during corporate prayer, he spoke—clearly and unequivocally! He said, in the way that he speaks prophetically in keeping with his Word, *"I am a jealous God!"*

The only thing was, I am at pains to say, that the voice of our Lord was not recognized or honored in the way he spoke as an answer to our waiting and seeking. Indeed, this reinforced that a determination was already sealed by the powers that be and that our waiting and seeking as a house of prayer was without discernment and substance in practice.

Prophetically, I could sense the commotion of the marketplace in my spirit with the inability of the sellers and money changers to comprehend and come to grips with why Jesus overturned their tables. Yet his disciples, those who walked with him, in seeing this jealousy, "remembered that it is written: 'Zeal for your house will consume me'" (John 2:17).

When the love and grace of God are made known to us in such a deep and delivering way, leading us to freedom, should we then be blind to seeing that we have become enslaved again in any form, then in his jealousy for our love, God will awaken us to this, one way or the other, sooner or later. We need to understand, as he declares it, "The LORD your God, who is among you, is a jealous God" (Deuteronomy 6:14).

By this, God says, as he has said since the days of Moses, that what he has delivered his people from—other gods and their influence (in other words, oppression and fear in whatever form)—we are to remain free of in our surrender to and trust in the Lord. When we are truly born again, we are the Lord's! We therefore "Do not worship any other god, for the LORD, whose name is Jealous, is a jealous God" (Exodus 34:14).

The worship of any other god and its influence on us is recognized for what it is at its core by the focus it has us place on self-preservation. In other words, when we do what we do by the flesh—in our own strength—we do so in order to be in control and safe. This is contrary to faith and walking in step with the Spirit. "For whoever wants to save their life will lose it, but whoever loses their life for me will save it" (Luke 9:24).

Absolute Surrender

The Holy Spirit highlights this jealousy Jesus has for us as the members of his body. He is jealous for our love and what we have said is his—our life and lives corporately! Just as on the day we found grace in him, so he requires as our Savior and Lord, personally and corporately, for the rest of our days, absolute surrender. When we blindly go back on this, even without realizing that we do, he comes after us with the very love that made him want to die for us on the cross in the first place.

The death of when, wittingly or unwittingly, we walk in ways contrary to life in Jesus more than meets its match in the power of his love in our wandering. "For love is as strong as death, its jealousy unyielding as the grave. It burns like blazing fire, like a mighty flame. Many waters cannot quench love; rivers cannot sweep it away" (Song of Songs 8:6-7).

The pride of the world from which we were saved, that we can still accommodate as believers, extraordinarily and thankfully, we are yet given more grace to see.

> Anyone who chooses to be a friend of the world becomes an enemy of God. Or do you think the Scripture says without reason that he jealously longs for the spirit he has caused to dwell in us? But he gives us more grace. That is why Scripture says, "God opposes the proud but shows favor to the humble." (James 4:4-6)

Even a man of the world and a world leader as a king in his days learned, after being brought very low, declaring, "Now I, Nebuchadnezzar, praise and exalt and glorify the King of heaven, because everything he does is right and all his ways are just. And those who walk in pride he is able to humble" (Daniel 4:37).

Chapter 10

Crosswinds

God's love, wisdom, thoughts, and ways are profound! They are higher than ours! He teaches us these. Even at the point at which we personally yielded to his very great redeeming love and since or when we experience this happening to another, we see that "God is exalted in his power. Who is a teacher like him? Who has prescribed his ways for him, or said to him, 'You have done wrong?' … How great is our God—beyond our understanding!" (Job 36:22-23, 26)

Crosswinds in the natural, simply put, are not winds blowing behind us or coming directly toward us but winds blowing across the path of the direction in which we are going. These winds create turbulence and can be tolerated and resisted, to a point, or used to our advantage.

Spiritually speaking, winds of God that we are not with because we are resistant to them, not willing to change our direction, are ultimately to our disadvantage. A teachable heart recognizes that there is much about the kingdom of God, its King, and his higher ways that are yet to be learned and experienced. "He makes winds his messengers" (Psalm 104:4).

For as much as we have learned and witnessed, we do well when with childlike spirits we still take such a keen interest and delight in life and are fascinated by it. And even more so, we should delight in the One who is the source of life and its creator. Knowing him who is behind life in all that is good and sobering is surely the greatest quest.

To truly know him as he is to be known and as he would have us know him brings us to a place of rest. We are confident in his love and goodness and able to learn from him and grow in grace.

> Are you tired? Worn out? Burned out on religion? Come
> to me. Get away with me and you'll recover your life.
> I'll show you how to take a real rest. Walk with me and
> work with me—watch how I do it. Learn the unforced
> rhythms of grace. I won't lay anything heavy or ill-
> fitting on you. Keep company with me and you'll learn
> how to live freely and lightly. (Matthew 11:28-30 MSG)

God chose, with exceptions, the likes of most of us! He chose us just as he chose the disciples that he did, as "unschooled, ordinary men" (Acts 4:13), to be with him and represent him. Such are many of the called and chosen! As those chosen, we are as Paul was and as he spoke about regarding what the church is made up of: the foolish, weak, lowly, and despised things (1 Corinthians 1:26-31).

Having this grace as God's chosen and called to be with Jesus at rest outside the camp, we are conscious that the only warranted boast we have is in the Lord. Matthew Henry's commentary hits the mark in reference to Paul's declaration about these chosen ones and God's ways in the above Scripture. "He is a better judge than we what instruments and measures will best serve the purposes of his glory" (Matthew Henry, *Matthew Henry's Commentary on the New Testament*: Grand Rapids, Michigan: Baker Book House 1983, Volume 8, Page 11).

Toronto

It was at the outset of 1994 that the full strength of the first wind spoken of in chapter one came upon and blew across the church. That wind (coined "The Toronto Blessing" by the UK newspaper *The Sunday Telegraph*) was a wind, shaking, and bringing change with the purpose of preparing the church for these times into which we have entered.

Crosswinds, prophetically speaking, are winds contrary to the world and the flesh but are of God, as when Jesus walked the earth and the Spirit came at Pentecost, that reveal the power of the cross and resurrection of Jesus. Such a wind as those blew in and around 1994, and many more are now bearing down upon the church to blow upon and across us.

Rather than resist these, the church must recognize, learn from, and align itself with these winds of the Spirit. God's winds will blow, more often than not, in ways we have not known but in keeping with the reality of the love, grace, truth, and majesty of God in Christ.

The former winds by which we have genuinely sailed or soared in revivals, creating new movements and denominations, are either passing or being refined by fire. Something very new is happening! These new winds of the same Spirit that have blown upon the church at different times and seasons that are contrary to the winds of a religious spirit are, yes, beginning to blow across the church and the earth now.

These are intended, as much as anything, to impart fearless faith and courage among the members of the body, making known the pure fear of the Lord, love of God, and love for God and to know these in all their brilliance. These will bring a fresh and living "testimony of Jesus" (Revelation 1:2, 9; 19:10).

The wind of Toronto was unique and not surprisingly produced vast reactions and responses to it. It was truly a blessing and indeed a test! It exposed, as much as anything, the religious spirit. These same spiritual winds of the Spirit, both now here and yet coming, will likewise (but with even greater mass and velocity) prove to be a blessing, testing, life-changing, and rattling in their nature and intensity, to the core, as when Jesus walked the earth and Pentecost came.

Discerning the Lord

What it was truly like in those days in which our Lord Jesus walked this earth in embodying and carrying such a different wind and sense about him, in contrast to the status quo of the Pharisees, Sadducees, and teachers of the law, was dramatic. This was so dramatic that much of what had been understood and expected about the coming of the Messiah was other than was thought and better understood in its unfolding.

There are encouraging exceptions to the rule among those who did not foresee or recognize the Lord, as best as one could foresee, with those who did discern the times and the "rising sun" (Luke 1:78).

Among these were Simeon and Anna. Note well what is said about these righteous, devout, and prophetically sensitive ones.

Note their relationship with the Lord, sensitivity to the Spirit, sense of expectancy, and ability to receive grace in the way he came. Humility enables us to receive! They discerned God in the form he came—as a child. They were given grace to do this because of their own humility of heart. They trusted in God to be as good as God truly is. They were led to him and saw him whom they always looked to. They recognized in spirit the One they knew!

> Simeon ... was waiting for the consolation of Israel ...
> It had been revealed to him by the Holy Spirit that he
> would not die before he had seen the Lord's Messiah.
> Moved by the Spirit ... Simeon took him in his arms
> and praised God ...
>
> Anna ... she was very old ... she never left the
> temple ... coming up to them at that very moment, she
> gave thanks to God and spoke about the child to all who
> were looking forward to the redemption of Jerusalem.
> (Luke 2:25-38)

It was likewise no less spectacular when the disciples and those gathered at Pentecost and in the days of the early church following encountered the Lord in such a different form than what the people were accustomed to and expected. All alike (believers, those who did not yet believe, and the religious) witnessed God unlike they had ever truly known, except those who always looked to him.

Like David, there are those known for this: "I keep my eyes always on the LORD. With him at my right hand, I will not be shaken" (Psalm 16:8). These believers in the early church, with these eyes, discerned the form and ways in which he came and moved. They were not shaken. They already knew him, or at least did in some good measure—in their spirits, by the Spirit. "As it is written: 'What no eye has seen, what no ear has heard, and what no human mind has conceived'—the things God has prepared for those who love him—these are the things God has revealed to us by his Spirit" (1 Corinthians 2:9-10).

Dramatic Changes

Returning to the church is a sense of awe, reverence, and wonder that many experienced in those early days of the church (and at times since) through what instruments and measures the Lord chose that best served the purposes of his glory. Wonders and interesting things, as these few that I quote as follows, we will yet see in our day. We are in for dramatic changes in how we see the Lord, like the early church experienced.

The staggering, intoxicated-looking saints at the scene when the "sound like the blowing of a violent wind came" (Acts 2:2); the unsettling in the natural and spiritual when the threatened servants of the Lord prayed and "the place where they were meeting was shaken" (Acts 4:23-31); the "Great fear that seized the whole church and all who heard," because Ananias and his wife, Sapphira, had lied to the Holy Spirit with fatal consequences (Acts 5:1-11).

The many signs and wonders performed among the people, and yet "No one else dared joined them, even though they were highly regarded by the people," though paradoxically, "Nevertheless, more and more men and women believed in the Lord and were added to their number" (Acts 5:12-14); the taken-aback look on faces gathered when "people brought the sick into the streets and laid them on beds and mats so that at least Peter's shadow might fall on some of them as he passed by" (Acts 5:15).

In the context of recognizing signs and wonders being from God (as wonderful things indeed and things that leave us wondering), whatever these may have truly looked like on the ground, we are also left wondering, along with what is recorded, what else may have happened. "Jesus did many other things as well. If every one of them were written down, I suppose that even the whole world would not have room for the books that would be written" (John 21:25). This is extraordinary, to say the least! The bottom line is that we must recognize the Lord, walk with him, and learn from him, whatever happens.

We are at a crossroads in our experience, understanding, and faith with these crosswinds at hand. The landscape of the church is truly in for dramatic change. God has designed the church to know change—though again, not in what makes the church the church. He has created the church to be an instrument of change, even as we have been redeemed and changed.

"In Him we live and move" (Acts 17:28). What is behind our living and moving is of the same foundation on which we were born again. Spirit and wind go hand in hand! As with the natural wind, we cannot determine the where, when, or how of the Spirit wind. Yet we know something is happening and is life-changing, and this is not limited to the time of our salvation. "The wind blows wherever it pleases. You hear its sound, but you cannot tell where it comes from or where it is going. So it is with everyone born of the Spirit" (John 3:8).

There are those who look on when someone is born again, even with all the good fruit that comes from it, yet have no real understanding. They shrug their shoulders as though it were a passing fad. Interestingly too, many of the Lord's people did not recognize or discern the reason for the crosswind and whirlwind of Toronto that came over and across the church, coming upon the beach as from the Lord. Some saw this whole mess as a distraction needing to be set in order, like earth-moving equipment used in uselessly seeking to put the beach back to what was familiar and what looked clean and tidy to those doing it.

A Change of Heart

Of the authentic and welcome changes deep within the hearts and lives of those impacted by Toronto in the early to mid-nineties, as with those in the early church, there was much rejection of, resistance to, and railing against it. This was so, even in how I have described the opposition to the wind in the dream of chapter one.

A form of godliness proved to be more valuable and safe than the power of relationship with God and one another. This is what the early church powerfully experienced, both in blessing and opposition. This was, as much as anything, likewise what Toronto did in revealing and changing hearts. The religious spirit loathes change that exposes its control by flesh. Again, that we would see this is a grace to help us change our ways and walk in the Way.

Opposition and resistance come even when the fruit of such moves are evident, as in Saul's case. Saul, like religious believers in our days who encounter the Lord in a similar deeply personal and sometimes dramatic way, knew that his life had changed from the inside out by no other than the Lord. I have witnessed firsthand a friend and elder of a church transformed from having a Saul-like intransigence into an altogether different man of God. Gentleness replaced harshness, understanding replaced intolerance, and humility replaced pride. It was extraordinary, remarkable, and welcome!

Among the most outstanding features for those who were intensely impacted by the blessing of Toronto in those days was the way in which they were confronted with an altogether new and fresh revelation of God's love as a Father. With their generation for the most part having known so shallow a love being expressed demonstratively in their relationships with their earthly fathers, this was profound and healing, to say the least.

Toronto helped pave the way for today, producing godly and mature spiritual fathers, overseeing and strengthening churches, and raising up mature believers in their security in God our Father's lavishing love. "See what great love the Father has lavished on us, that we should be called children of God! And that is what we are!" (1 John 3:1)

Toronto heralded (as did Brownsville and Lakeland, among others, as forerunners) a profound change coming upon the landscape of the church. These have indeed paved and prepared the way for the Lord to move as he is and yet will in bringing a deep maturity to the members of the body and a great harvest into the kingdom.

The way is being made straight to recognize that what Jesus gave as gifts to the church for the equipping and maturity of the body have not passed but are now still so in order that Jesus would be revealed through his body preceding his return in all his glory.

> But to each one of us grace has been given as Christ apportioned it … So Christ himself gave the apostles, the prophets, the evangelists, the pastors and teachers, to equip his people for works of service, so that the body of Christ may be built up, until we all reach unity in the faith and in the knowledge of the Son of God and become mature, attaining to the whole measure of the fullness of Christ. (Ephesians 4:7, 11-13)

This unity, maturity, and whole measure of the church is where we are going in a way that the early church began to experience but was always intended to attain with us. "These were all commended for their faith, yet none of them received what had been promised, since God had planned something better for us so that only together with us would they be made perfect" (Hebrews 11:39-40). With this reality in the wind (as crosswinds) in these days, as much as back then, there is resistance to it now.

The opposing religious winds and the pressure of them in the way they have deceived the church since the early church (let alone beforehand) will not prevail. Their craftiness and deception are being exposed by the grace given to the church thanks to the winds of the Spirit, especially since Toronto.

With this grace that Christ has given, coming of age,

> Then we will no longer be infants, tossed back and forth by the waves, and blown here and there by every wind of teaching and by the cunning and craftiness of people in their deceitful scheming. Instead, speaking the truth in love, we will grow to become in every respect the mature body of him who is the head, that is, Christ. From him the whole body, joined and held together by every supporting ligament, grows and builds itself up in love, as each part does its work. (Ephesians 4:14-16)

Toronto was a wind that hit the religious spirit in the church head-on. The reason for the manifestation of barking as a result of that wind was symbolic of the exposure of the growling religious spirit that had both infiltrated the church and replaced the fear of the Lord with a fear of people. "Fear of man will prove to be a snare, but whoever trusts in the LORD is kept safe" (Proverbs 29:25).

The legacy of Toronto's blessing also had a deeply personal impact upon the displacement of our heads to keep them from ruling over our hearts. Those for whom Toronto was not God usually saw it that way because their heads blocked their hearts altogether. It is, however, the mind controlled by the Spirit that determines our assessment of all things, including any move of God, and not the Spirit barred by the limit of the understanding of our minds. Therefore, let the heart govern the mind of the body! "Trust in the LORD with all your heart and lean not on your own understanding … Above all else, guard your heart, for everything you do flows from it" (Proverbs 3:5, 4:23).

Toronto was instrumental and a sign to the body to prepare the way for the Lord to come in forms that are both old and new, similar and different from the forms in which we have become so accustomed. If it is the Lord we want, let's welcome him in who and by what please him. "He is a better judge than we what instruments and measures will best serve the purposes of his glory" (Matthew Henry, *Matthew Henry's Commentary on the New Testament:* Grand Rapids, Michigan: Baker Book House 1983, Volume 8, Page 11).

An Undivided Heart

Before I knew that this wind at the outset of 1994 was occurring, I experienced the reality of it coming upon me very deeply and personally. It turned the world I knew upside-down and the God I knew right-side-up.

Nine months beforehand, though, just shortly after Passover (Easter) in April 1993, the Lord set aside a time and place in which he led me to call upon him. It was both an exceptional and very personal time before the Lord. The summary of the deeply expressed desire of my heart was, "Teach me your way, LORD, that I may rely on your faithfulness; give me an undivided heart, that I may fear your name" (Psalm 86:11).

Where I was to find my life going as a consequence of that unforgettable time "out bush" (as we Aussies put it) proved to be both immensely painful in its brokenness and tremendously strengthening in its purpose. Those days are described in more detail in the following chapter.

The crosswind I was to encounter aligned the course of life in a way that my heart deeply longed for and sought. I am very grateful for the blessing of the crosswind(s).

Chapter 11

A Journey of Humility

Returning from Canberra to Adelaide in September 1997, I came to within twenty-five to thirty kilometers (fifteen to eighteen miles) of Narrandera in New South Wales on the Wagga Wagga side of town. I pulled over to the side of the road in the late afternoon, and I stayed there for the next two nights. I was in my old but reliable car, which far from being loaded up to the roof, housed my few and necessary worldly possessions.

I was on the road for the seventeen months since April 1996 when I departed from Bendigo, Victoria. This was my calling in being wherever I understood the Lord would have me to be to minister what I understood the Holy Spirit was saying to the church across the board. This was an apprenticeship of faith in knowing the One who is the Word. "I will instruct you and teach you in the way you should go; I will counsel you with my loving eye on you" (Psalm 32:8).

Through the blessing and kindness of family, friends, brothers, and sisters in the Lord, I was accommodated in those days—at times simply overnight and in other cases for somewhat longer periods. Just as often (and probably more often), my car, a medium-sized sedan, was my mobile home. An exception was the six months during which I rented a house in Eden Hills in Adelaide in late 1997 through mid-1998. It was at that point after Eden Hills I returned on a third trip to Tasmania to minister and where I found myself remaining and calling home thereafter.

Before coming to the place in pulling up on the side of the road outside Narrandera in September 1997, the journey of the heart in life to that point, especially since the very outset of 1994, was both totally sobering and richly life-giving.

Before I come back to share the dream I had two nights after pulling up where I did, I will provide some further context for that dream. (It is fitting that some of what I write about here I do in a car parked by a beach.)

Deep Calling to Deep

At the very beginning of 1994, before commencing my third year at Bible College of Victoria (BCV), as it was then called, without any prior warning or expectation it was to happen, my wife left me, taking our two children with her. In sparing you any further unnecessary details for the purpose of staying on the page of where this is going, within a year, without her looking back, I was divorced.

What made this even more painful was the reality that this was my second failed marriage. To a man who sought to know, love, and serve the Lord and grow in grace, the grief and ache in my heart was as deep as it could go. I remembered that I had asked the Lord nine months before this valley of the shadow of death that he would show me his ways and give me an "undivided heart" (Psalm 86:11). What sense did this all make of my desire to serve the Lord and his church with the truth now exposed of my failures (those real and those without basis) and the hope held out in the gospel?

This place of ocean-deep sorrow, ironically, marked the beginning of what perhaps I could best describe as encountering in spirit the experience that Jonah had in finding life out of death. I can relate to what Jonah prayed.

> In my distress I called to the LORD, and he answered me. From deep in the realm of the dead I called for help, and you listened to my cry ... The engulfing waters threatened me, the deep surrounded me; seaweed was wrapped around my head. To the roots of the mountains I sank down; the earth beneath barred me in forever.

But you, LORD my God, brought my life up from the
pit. (Jonah 2:2, 5-6)

The sting and the remedy, the bitterness and the sweetness, and
the depths and the heights in which the Lord revealed himself in and
through those days became a watershed for and foundation in knowing
God as life itself and Jesus as Savior, Lord over all, and friend. What's
more, during those days, the Holy Spirit bathed me with such comfort
and reassurance while revealing all that I needed to see about myself
that I could not keep.

I could never have known that the desire I sought in going to
college in the first place, to know and to serve the Lord better, would
be fulfilled in such a sifting, severe, disciplining, and exposing manner.
The theology I would come away with when I left BCV in early 1996
was not of the head but of the heart, "written not with ink but with the
Spirit of the living God, not on tablets of stone but on tablets of human
hearts" (2 Corinthians 3:3).

Without exaggeration, for the first six and a half months following
the separation, not a day went by in which I did not at some given point
cry or weep from the core of my being. The hot tears unplugged from
the well of the deepest part of my soul and ran like an overflowing
stream down my face, day and night.

An Indelible and Endurable Mark

On a particular occasion, as I sat in the college library in those
days, I found that I didn't have an ounce of strength of spirit left in me
and next to none physically. I lacked the ability to concentrate on my
studies, for all hope I had as I could see it at that moment was sapped,
and I was completely numb.

In that raw reality I found myself facing, I was left without the
capacity at the time to comprehend the place my life had come to and
where the Lord was in it all. I am very grateful for the "advocate to help
you and be with you forever" (John 14:16) who gave me grace to trust
in the Lord with all my heart and not lean on my own understanding,
weak as my heart seemed in that demanding void of nothingness. I got

up from my desk with what little physical strength I could muster. I walked toward my car to drive back to the small caravan (trailer) that was home in my brother's driveway.

As I walked across the gravel college car park, I experienced a grace of insight that has left an indelible and endurable mark on my life. It came to me as I took one courageous step in front of another just to go on and not simply, exhausted, lie down there and then, with my spirit faded so low and lifelessness looming so very near and real.

In that moment, I saw and sensed within my spirit, from the Spirit, two vastly contrasting scenes between our enemies' loathing and our Father's exceedingly more powerful and unfailing love. Such insights into the spiritual realm as this, behind the scenes of the natural, come overlaying the natural eyes by the eyes of our spirits. In this case, the two scenes came, remarkably, at one and the same time.

Such eye-opening evidence as this in seeing in spirit the very real spiritual battle in which we are engaged and the fortressed protection afforded in it is among one of the most encouraging and outstanding gifts that we do well to recognize is from the Lord. This grace that the body has been given, the church cannot strategically and confidently march without.

I saw myself face-down on the ground of the car park with my head turned to the left side. The Devil had his boot on my neck, twisting his foot back and forth. With no small amount of force, he did this with my head pushed hard against the harsh gravel stones underneath me. His attitude and intent were obvious enough. His disdain was loud and intense. His enmity was as deep a darkness as I have ever known.

With that chilling, demanding verdict and merciless sentence, I could see and feel myself losing the hold I had of our heavenly Father's hand. The anguish that came with this sense of helplessness in no longer being able to hold on was dreadful. I really don't know how else to describe or convey what the pain of losing your grip on life as you've only ever known it was like.

The weight and length of that moment were excruciating. Without being able to do anything about the unbearable loss I felt, with the sense of life slipping away, I resigned myself in surrender to what was beyond my ability to remedy. Then, as sure as day follows night and joy follows mourning, what was out of my hands completely turned around as I saw the hand of God taking hold of mine. His grip was strong yet gentle, remarkably tender in its deliverance, and profoundly assuring.

With this, he communicated to me in a way that was spirit-to-spirit, even as "God is spirit" (John 4:24). He said, "You have always thought that it was your hold of me that held you and keeps you. But it has always been my hold of you that does!"

The truth and power of the following Scripture of God's love in his Son came alive and is very real to me as a result of that earthed in life spiritual experience. "My sheep listen to my voice; I know them, and they follow me. I give them eternal life, and they shall never perish; no one will snatch them out of my Father's hand. I and the Father are one" (John 10:27-28).

The Lord Is Good

That unforgettable day stands alongside other points, signs, and memorial stones of grace and equally impacting times. These accumulated riches have been gathered and treasured on a journey of humility. Truly, the Lord is good—the Holy and Righteous One—the way, truth, and life who said, "The thief comes only to steal and kill and destroy; I have come that they may have life, and have it to the full" (John 10:10).

The twenty years since have not diminished this towering time of my life with the events of those days. I call it a towering time because for as deep as the pain was and as dark the valley was, so much greater has been the mountain of grace, forgiveness, and getting to know the Lord intimately and his ways better.

I have come to understand perfectly well and very personally what Jesus spoke about regarding the woman who anointed him when he said, "I tell you, her sins—and they are many—have been forgiven, so she has shown me much love. But a person who is forgiven little shows only little love" (Luke 7:47 NLT).

We Live by Faith

As I parked there for those two nights outside of Narrandera in September 1997, I encountered a further (and often enough known) intense period of spiritual warfare. I did the best that I understood how to be strong and stand firm in the Lord and in the power of his might.

On the third day, I felt released to drive into Narrandera. By the time late afternoon and early evening arrived, I was totally exhausted. As a climax to the prolonged battle over those days before, on that day, I experienced a deep sense of sorrow with the hostile loathing of the opposition in spirit I faced. With next to no strength to go on, I pulled up in a parking area of the Mobil station on the edge of town and soon fell asleep. During the course of my sleep, I had a dream from the Lord.

I was in my car, just as I was when I had gone to sleep, but in a location that represented the journey in life that had gotten me where I was. My younger brother turned up, and as I got out of my car, I joyfully laughed about the water that had leaked between the windscreen and the top of the dashboard, working its way down behind the dashboard to the floor of the driver's side.

I began pouring the water out of the foot of my sleeping bag to show him what life was like for me. It was so funny to me. I had no care in the world about things being this way, the difficulties that came with life as it was, and the foolishness that this seemed to others. I was not ashamed! I was overjoyed being in God our Father's will, living, and in serving him as a son is honored to do.

Just after this, I started to walk with my brother a few steps. I found I had reason to brush my hair with my hand, conscious that something was lurking in it, though I had no fear of it. When I flicked the very spot where I sensed that something was, it turned out to be a spider that dropped to the ground and began moving off.

The spider was large and very unique in appearance. It symbolically represented witchcraft. It was the spirit and nature behind the battle I had experienced that past day and over those past days outside Narrandera. Witchcraft is a spirit that seeks to manipulate, dominate, and control. The conflict I had encountered over those days and the dream I had with this spider in it gave me insight into what was happening and wisdom for how to respond.

Even as the spider raced away from me in the dream, yet only to soon come across it again, there was a precious and powerful sense of peace, joy, and unity in the atmosphere. Along with my brother, I sensed my mother present, though only in spirit, because she had already gone to be with the Lord (earlier the year before in March 1996).

That I could sense her in this way represented as much as anything, the legacy of her life and godly influence, in the context of what were often extremely difficult circumstances for us as a family.

I had not known such a great and rich sense of peace, joy, and unity in our spirits to that extent before in the natural or spiritual realm. And it happened "in the presence of my enemies" (Psalm 23:5).

At the same time as this, my brother (and mother) beckoned me for something that I had. They did this with grace and without inferring any impatience in their urging determination to draw something out of me. Without them actually saying what it was, I came to understand that it was faith. This was a crucial message, for faith was a pillar in our history as a family.

Faith, in spiritual warfare, is wisdom, vital, and indispensable. For along with the other equipment required in this very real, sobering, yet exhilarating spiritual battle in which we are engaged, we are charged, "In addition to all this, take up the shield of faith, with which you can extinguish all the flaming arrows of the evil one" (Ephesians 6:16). (Note the word "all.")

The next thing in the dream that I knew, was that I was back in the car by myself, but this time, the car was where I was actually parked in Narrandera. When in the car, I came across the spider again. I went to hit it boldly with something. But it was in an awkward spot. When I did try to hit it, it cunningly darted out of sight to hide itself.

After trying to sort out the spider in this way, I realized immediately that I could not deal with it in that kind of way. I was given to understand that it had no real substance to it and was harmless to one walking by faith. I knew by this that though it would continue to lurk about, it held no fear for me at that time or ever. I awoke out of the dream at that point.

Angels

Immediately upon waking, I heard very distinctively and clearly a song I knew that an old godly friend and seasoned warrior wrote about angels' wings. This greatly assured me that in what I had encountered and in every very real spiritual battle to come—in foolishness, weakness, humility, and despising—angelic companions were at work and at hand. "Are not all angels ministering spirits sent to serve those who will inherit salvation?" (Hebrews 1:14)

I was made aware with this song from the Lord in the context it came that the presence of angels—ministering spirits—play a key role in serving the chosen and called and those born for battle. The sense of the presence of angels upon awaking out of this dream and battle provided a tangible and assuring sense of love, acceptance, and watchfulness from the Lord.

The Lord's presence was striking in the way in which he was there through these emissaries. The strongest senses I felt in spirit were calm, peace, and reassurance. This was truly indicative of what angels brought and spoke throughout Scripture time and time again, saying, "Do not be afraid."

God Chose

As I continued to sit there upon awaking, soaking up the encouragement of it all, I heard spoken into the core of my spirit, as clearly as I have ever heard the Spirit speak, this Scripture: "God chose the foolish things … the weak things … the lowly things of this world and the despised things—and the things that are not—to nullify the things that are, so that no one may boast before him" (1 Corinthians 1:27-29).

Grace comes packaged, as it were, in this way—even as Jesus came! While thinking about all this as I fuelled up and went on my way with this light, in the darkness of the night in which I traveled, I was then reminded of what I had also been awoken to the previous morning. "For it has been granted to you on behalf of Christ not only to believe in

Him, but also to suffer for Him" (Philippians 1:29). Grace and suffering are inextricably linked!

> "My grace is sufficient for you, for my power is made perfect in weakness." Therefore I will boast all the more gladly about my weaknesses, so that Christ's power may rest on me. That is why, for Christ's sake, I delight in weaknesses, in insults, in hardships, in persecutions, in difficulties. For when I am weak, then I am strong. (2 Corinthians 12:9-10)

"He guides the humble in what is right and teaches them his way" (Psalm 25:9).

Chapter 12

Dismantling the God Box

Upon awaking in the natural, whether immediately preceding, at, or very shortly after awaking, this is a time known for when the Lord communicates. Often enough, what he communicates is a song. That song may well be what draws us to worship our amazing God and his glorious Son in praise at the outset of the day. That song could just as well, however, be one in which we hear as a song over us to strengthen and hold us in the Lord's great and unfailing love.

A song may well be what we hear. Yet it is also a unique time out of rest from which we just as likely hear from the Lord in him revealing and making something known to us. That something could be from or in keeping with his Word. It might be that we are being made aware of what could well be before us on that given day or about someone or something to pray and intercede about.

The attention the Lord draws us to at such a time as that, as he also does at other times, is valuable when we know that this comes from him. So when the Lord spoke to me in such a way on the morning of Friday, October 12, 2012 and did so in an especially loud or amplified way, I took notice, as he would have us do. That he did on that particular date was not for the first time. He had done it before. He does that!

Major Changes

There are times and dates on the calendar that the Lord marks out and has set in place to be especially heard in communicating what is on his heart. And while the Lord always speaks in one fashion, shape, form, or another, there are times in which a trumpet sounds, announcing a timely message that calls us to sit up and take particular note. This awaking on that morning was what that was like. The Spirit of Jesus conveyed to me with sharpness and clearly that there were major changes occurring in the body (the church) at that time.

The way in which I heard this and the timing of it was like being charged as a soldier to stand to attention. It truly came as a trumpet sounding to make ready. It was an alert and a summons that a necessary shift and move was taking place spiritually, having significance on the ground in the life of the Lord's people. I was aware in a way that one simply is, when there is a sense of something like this happening, that it had connection to a specific thing. In this case, I just knew it had a relationship to the God box.

In the months preceding, the Lord had Ray, a good friend and brother in the Lord, prophetically attend to and deal with the God box. The God box is the container and restriction that we personally, as well as the church corporately, have built to accommodate God. Ray prophetically held in hand the dismantling tool, breaking and smashing the God box that had been crafted for that prophetic occasion. By this, God says that he wants to move in our lives and his church without restriction and containment.

Rob, another dear brother, and I listened to Ray share about the way he had originally received the sense of this prophetically striking experience. He did this as we sat over morning tea in fellowship at Constitution Dock in Hobart in the months preceding the act of dismantling the God box, as well as the trumpet charge I heard on October 12, 2012. As he did, Rob and I felt such a compelling gravity on the necessity for Ray to actually perform this act as a sign in the natural of the spiritual change at hand in these days.

I will never forget those moments in fellowship together with the moving sense about this sign to and for the church. Rob and I could only look at each other and be deeply impressed by the Lord as we listened on. This came in a way that I have never experienced before in having such a witness with another—in a way that you know that this is something from the Lord and that it absolutely must be done.

The Axe Falls

This commissioned prophetic act carried out by Ray at a Kingdom's Call gathering of believers from across the church in Tasmania happened at Trinity Anglican Church in Strahan on Tasmania's West Coast on the evening of Wednesday, September 17, 2012.

On the Monday evening before and as a kickoff for those days together, we experienced a most exceptional and exceedingly special time in worship. Two brothers in the Lord, as worship leaders, who had not accompanied each other before (or met prior to the occasion), led us under the anointing of the Spirit where neither they nor we had gone before. There is no doubt that praise and worship of such unique character in its prophetic substance had a deep connection to where we were going with the God box.

The representative God box the size of an apple crate (not the larger apple bin) had been crafted for the occasion by a local minister and man of God. At the given time, after he clarified what this was all about, Ray took an axe to the God box and dismantled it. He did a good job of it! The Lord removes the restrictions and containment we have placed on him. His kingdom and ways are vastly greater than such limits. "Unless the LORD builds the house, the builders labor in vain" (Psalm 127:1).

The major changes occurring in these last days, in as much as anything, are to deliver the church from any imprisoning culture, structures, and traditions based on fear and pride that contain and limit the Spirit of grace. We are being made to see together, as we saw so evidently when we met our Savior, that "When pride comes, then comes disgrace, but with humility comes wisdom" (Proverbs 11:2).

Hope of Glory

Following that evening breakfast I had, spoken of in chapter five, as an added witness to the dawning new day for the church, Tina Maree and I knew that we were to transition from that which was passing to that which was coming. Whenever the cloud moves, it's time to move.

We were to soon see the Spirit leading the way for us to leave Tasmania in June 2003 and park for eighteen months in Sydney. There, we were blessed, refreshed, stretched, and re-equipped. Our time and fellowship at DaySpring Church (a fitting name for a new day) was to ground us in the grace that we have come to so deeply value.

On our return at the very outset of 2005 to Tassie (as we Aussies call Tasmania), we established the ministry of Shiloh in Ulverstone at first and then Shiloh Fellowship Church at Port Sorell. After three years and following on from ministering in different parts of Australia out of the download released during the days of Lakeland in mid-2008, our God box was dismantled. How this occurred and what this meant was a huge lesson in learning in a fresh way—what going from glory to glory can mean when it seems like anything but glory.

It was at the time of that juncture in early October 2008 that I was with our good friends from, again fittingly, Hope of Glory church in South Yarra (bordering Prahran), Melbourne. Though I didn't see it at the time, as we often enough don't, the reality was that the Lord was taking off the lid in our lives, even as he does in his church corporately across the earth.

The lid on the container of grace and truth, comes off so that we see Jesus as he is in us and walk in what we have in him. "Christ in you, the hope of glory. He is the one we proclaim, admonishing and teaching everyone with all wisdom, so that we may present everyone fully mature in Christ" (Colossians 1:27-28).

At that time and back at home, Tina Maree and I awoke together, sat up in bed, and looked at each other, sharing an unusual sense out of which we said precisely the same thing to each other, "We can't do this anymore!" We knew this to mean that we were to no longer continue the ministry and church in the form it was, truly good as it was. We were being called from glory to glory.

We had been obedient to the Spirit in establishing Shiloh. We had no expectation that the Lord would call us to lay it down. However, to hang on to what we had to let go would be to do the very opposite of how we began in obedience! The surrender of our lives and obedience to the Lord of all, whatever that looks like, he is very worthy of. So it took the same obedience when the Spirit led us in our beginning as it did with our ending. The church truly is the Lord's, not ours. Does the Lord shut his church down? Well, no—and yes!

Whenever the Lord of glory prepares to raise something up to reveal his glory in a new way, a letting go or dismantling of what that was for a time must make way for the surpassing glory to come.

We weren't able to see at that time, however, what was to come in how that would look. We just knew that we loved the Lord and sought to be obedient, whatever the personal cost. Testing would surely come, as it did and must do. It brings humility, produces grace, imparts maturity, and makes for life and growth. We are equipped through this necessity to change. This is why the re-landscaping of the church is so worth it, as difficult but as blessed as the process is and as life-giving and joy-releasing as the birth pains prove.

Letting Go

A boomerang (an Australian aboriginal tool that when thrown returns to the thrower) was given to me during those days as a birthday present from the Lord through a sister in Christ. There was a sure prophetic promise with this that if I were to let the boomerang of our ministry as we thought of it to go, it would surely return in the Lord's time and way. We were not to realize this return (the good investment of surrender) for another four and a half years.

It was at that stage also that a friend and sister who had been in fellowship with us at Shiloh had a dream. Simply put, while being with us where we lived, someone close to her and somewhat older passed away right in front of her, slowly, progressively, and literally out of sight. She deeply mourned this loss of what was. Then a beautiful young blond girl of five who was our daughter rose up and came forth right where there was loss. As we watched on as proud parents, this child brought great comfort to our friend.

The loss with Shiloh was real. While Shiloh was already out of the box in good measure, it was still a God box in terms of where we were compared to where we were going and what needed to pass on. It was a profoundly testing time indeed, personally and for Tina Maree, in more ways than one. But there was grace! A job came up seamlessly for Tina Maree in administration at a Christian school. That was back in Ulverstone to where our hearts were still drawn, as they were at the outset of 2005. And so we went, and there we are to this day.

Ultimately, we found ourselves in fellowship where we least expected we would be led and land (see chapter nine in the section subtitled "A Snapshot"). This was a setting as church like I had known most of my life.

To be back there and from whence we came was a welcome refinement of the grace that comes from the humility that is needed for the body to recognize the body and love one another where we're at. This leading of the Lord was where we were more than happy to fellowship—to love and serve him and his body there. An additional immense blessing and grace in going back both to Ulverstone and this familiar setting was the new and precious friends we found and made there.

During those days also in June 2010 (as spoken of already in chapter six), among other most encouraging gifts, was Kingdom's Call, a ministry we were blessed to establish and oversee. It set a benchmark in my heart in service to the King in calling his people together from near and far. It heralded, in rest and peace, to arise and shine with the glory at hand that many of God's people throughout the earth have sensed and are being thoroughly prepared for.

A Free Life

I was both amazed and pleasantly surprised when I awoke one morning in May 2012 to hear the Holy Spirit say, "Galatians 5:1, *The Message*." It reads, "Christ has set us free to live a free life. So take your stand! Never again let anyone put a harness of slavery on you."

If that wasn't enough to grab hold of my attention, which it was, it pierced my heart even more so in the best possible sense when a message centered on that same Scripture and version of the Word of God was spoken within weeks on June 10, 2012. Illustrated with this word was a picture of a kookaburra (an Australian bird and icon that has a unique laugh) that was, incredibly, literally seen caged on the speaker's way to church. Nobody cages a kookaburra!

The speaker's name, by the way, was Stephen. This is most fitting! He then said, "We wanna move from being a kookaburra trapped in a steel cage to being an eagle that locks our wings and soars on the grace and freedom of God."

What made this story even more pertinent, apart from the Galatians 5:1 word, was that a kookaburra has long held unique symbolism in my heart. This came about in August 1999. Following on from a number of days in which many of the Lord's people from across the church in Australia gathered in Canberra, the nation's capital, an all-night prayer vigil was held for those desiring to stay on for it. I was encouraged by just how many did!

The number of those who attended was such that we were broken up into what I recall was at least five different groups as we each rotated certain strategic locations around Canberra.

At the crack of that fresh dawn on Saturday, we all regrouped for our final intercessory push. We met around Australia's Federation Stone between the old and new parliament houses in our nation's seat of government.

An Australian Christian aboriginal elder (since gone ahead to be with the Lord) was, appropriately and fittingly, charged with speaking and prophetically declaring on our behalf what the Spirit led him to say and do. He did this as he literally mounted the Stone (as only such a man of his authority could get away with). In the course of his unction, under the anointing, as he proclaimed "Arise, Shine, for your light has come" (Isaiah 60:1-3), a kookaburra came nearby and bellowed out its iconic laugh. I was stunned!

This was profound in symbolic power! It is to be well noted that when in Australia, if that sound is heard, as the Lord's people we are to be aware and pay attention to this glorious prophetic summons and kingdom's call, for "the glory of the LORD rises upon you" (Isaiah 60:1).

So when I heard of a caged kookaburra, of all things, in the context of "Christ has set us free to live a free life" (Galatians 5:1), you could well appreciate my attention. However, the God box of that steel cage, in resisting the call, has been prophetically dismantled, and major changes are at hand.

The God box of imprisoning restraint is passing! The grace of a free life to live out from under and within a religious impoverished spirit has been purchased. There has come a re-landscaping of our seeing!

The day has come to rise up, shine, and see the Lord, you, and others differently. We can truly live in the fellowship of the Spirit as family and as warriors together in the battle of the good fight of the faith and soar on wings like eagles with the winds of the Spirit as sons and daughters of the Way.

Chapter 13

Victorious

The spiritual parents of the maturing sons and daughters of the church have the honor of paving the way of grace and peace. A prophetic perspective of this wisdom and humility in the church is with the transition and changing of the guard, as when athletes pass a baton in a relay race from one to the other.

The kingdom team of those who serve one another in love and for God's glory in this way "will be able to boast on the day of Christ that I did not run or labor in vain" (Philippians 2:16). These are the truly victorious!

When God transitions the great work of his kingdom from one generation to another and from glory to glory, the new is still his work but with a different face and taste. Scripture affirms it. Our experience of life in families recognizes this, and the wise discern it so.

The new is rising yet does not have the advantage that the old does. As Jesus said, "new wine must be poured into new wineskins. And no one after drinking the old wine wants the new, for they say, 'The old is better'" (Luke 5:38-39). It is crucial for that which was not to become proud over that which now is. The old is good, but the old, when it was new, had grace to become the better old.

The wisdom of the wise teachers and sages who have gone before and those now being called to forerun dispense the value of the treasures of what was, what is, and what is to come, for "a disciple in the kingdom of heaven is like the owner of a house who brings out of his storeroom new treasures as well as old" (Matthew 13:52).

The "good old" that we have known has had the honor of forerunning and is applauded and saluted accordingly. The new in its new wineskin (with comments from the old, like, "Wow, that's—um, different!") sets its face toward the goal to win the prize, as did its predecessor. They, likewise, find their acceptance not in the accolades of the approval of people but the reward of having heard in the quietness of his or her heart, and on that day, the approval of God.

In transition at the handover on the runner's track, there comes a point at which the one holding the baton gives over his or her hard-fought responsibility. As the baton passes hands, the first runner says, in effect, "Go for it!" The athlete taking hold of the baton shares the common and focused goal and responds, saying in effect, "Thank you!"

The spiritual parents who have gone before and are still alive are to be valued, esteemed, and honored. They yet have much to contribute with wisdom, skills, and experience. However, God's intention is that these dear ones would not be an impediment or stumbling block to the Lord's ways by exasperating (embittering) their spiritual children by holding out or holding back on them.

The sons and daughters must be given grace, space, and encouragement to step up, race, and soar without their ways being blocked, barred, or tied down as the wind blows, even as it is. Otherwise, these children will lose heart, even as many already have (and gone); yet the Lord is good. "The righteous cry out, and the LORD hears them; he delivers them from all their troubles. The LORD is close to the brokenhearted and saves those who are crushed in spirit" (Psalm 34:17–18).

Even as in a natural family, once one is an aged parent or grandparent, these precious ones lay aside holding the fort and in humility hand over responsibility and oversight to their beloved children. They maintain all the honor that is theirs for having paved the way.

These aging and blessed forebears cannot afford to walk in fear and undue pride. Such apprehension as that in not letting go is unhealthy and will likely cause unnecessary pain and anguish, let alone disruption to the power of inheritance.

The growth and strength of the church of the future, the church of the past can confidently entrust to its Head and walk in the peace that results from apprehending the wisdom that says, "Do not be anxious about anything" (Philippians 4:6).

Love One Another

Again, nothing that makes the beach a beach changes when its landscape is altered. All the elements are still there. The One who created it is called "Faithful and True" (Revelation 19:11). He will sustain it even as the church has been kept by the power of God all along. It is not going down the plughole!

The opposite is true! The church arises and shines because its light has come, and the glory of the Lord rises upon it, even as darkness covers the earth and thick darkness is over the people who know not their Creator, Savior, and Lord (Isaiah 60:1-2). The church is the means through which, when in step with the Holy Spirit, the world would know that God loves it. He does because he gave it and gives to it what demonstrates just how much he loves it—even his body! By this it would see, have the hope, and find the grace that it cannot truly live without.

Just as Jesus loves us and gives us life as life is to be really known, we come to him as we are, whoever we are, and wherever we are at. We are called to show this same love, acceptance, honor, and humility toward one another, and in doing so, make Jesus' love known.

The Spirit breathes freshly the charge Jesus gave, as when Jesus first spoke it. "A new command I give you: Love one another. As I have loved you so you must love one another. By this everyone will know that you are my disciples, if you love one another" (John 13:34-35).

"By this!"—by the grace that is ours in us knowing personally and deeply, as deep as deep can go, that we are loved and that there is no fear in this love. Our fellowship together in this truth, in just how truly amazing and great God's grace is in Jesus our Lord, is a fellowship in the love that he has for us for one another.

Our mission is to be real, as close to home as it gets, as much as we would be, as far away from home as we might be sent. This is the true missionary and apostolic church!

The love, humility, and honor we are to show are very down-to-earth and spiritual. We feed, shelter, clothe, care for, and identify with others in literal and spiritual ways as to the Lord.

> For I was hungry and you gave me something to eat, I was thirsty and you gave me something to drink, I was a stranger and you invited me in, I needed clothes and you clothed me, I was sick and you looked after me, I was in prison and you came to visit me. (Matthew 25:35-36)

The Battle Is the Lord's

The love of Christ and love for the Lord Jesus in these last days will be demonstrated in and through the church as powerfully as it ever has since the beginning. The battle Jesus won and Stephen encountered will be as close to home as it gets and as far away from home as we go.

This epic battle between life and death, trust and flesh, and peace and fear is coming into the light like never before. The bookends of history, with God revealing where we are, are evident. The legacy of the fall in the Garden, in us being seen as we are, is this: "I was afraid because I was naked; so I hid" (Genesis 3:10).

Consequently, we see and will see like we've never see so well the spirit of fear and death victoriously overcome by the spirit of faith and life, even when fear and death seek to silence that life. "Cain attacked his brother and killed him … 'What have you done? Listen! Your brother's blood cries out to me from the ground'" (Genesis 4:8, 10).

With the prophetic trumpet of grace with which Abel still speaks, so too, boldly and with the humility that comes from wisdom, the victorious, overcoming church is heard declaring and echoing grace and faith with a loud voice.

Even though "the great dragon, that ancient serpent called the devil, or Satan, who leads the whole world astray" (Revelation 12:9) is infuriated by the glory of the Lord and is exposed, "They triumphed over him by the blood of the Lamb and by the word of their testimony;

they did not love their lives so much as to shrink from death" (Revelation 12:11).

Every power of darkness bows to the truth that "Jesus Christ is Lord" (Philippians 2:11). Outside the camp, our focus is our Savior, not sin, fear, our adversary, or terror. This is the wind of the wisdom, humility and power of the church.

In every spiritual battle earthed in the reality of life in these last days, Jesus is Lord, our resting place, and our strength. As David declared it out of the apprenticeship and reality of the battle and as a corporate David will, "I love you, LORD, my strength." (Psalm 18:1).

Have Faith in God outside the Camp

> Now faith is confidence in what we hope for and assurance about what we do not see. This is what the ancients were commended for …
>
> Therefore, since we are surrounded by such a great cloud of witnesses, let us throw of everything that hinders and the sin that so easily entangles. And let us run with perseverance the race marked out for us, fixing our eyes on Jesus, the pioneer and perfecter of faith.
>
> For the joy set before him he endured the cross, scorning its shame, and sat down at the right hand of the throne of God. Consider him who endured such opposition from sinners, so that you will not grow weary and lose heart …
>
> But you have come to Mount Zion, to the city of the living God, the heavenly Jerusalem. You have come to thousands upon thousands of angels in joyful assembly, to the church of the firstborn, whose names are written in heaven.
>
> You have come to God, the Judge of all, to the spirits of the righteous made perfect, to Jesus the mediator of a new covenant, and to the sprinkled blood that speaks a better word than the blood of Abel.

See to it that you do not refuse him who speaks. If they did not escape when they refused him who warned them on earth, how much less will we, if we turn away from him who warns us from heaven? At that time his voice shook the earth, but now he has promised, "Once more I will shake not only the earth but also the heavens." The words "once more" indicate the removing of what can be shaken—that is, created things—so that what cannot be shaken may remain.

Therefore, since we are receiving a kingdom that cannot be shaken, let us be thankful, and so worship God acceptably with reverence and awe, for our "God is a consuming fire."

Let us, then, go to him outside the camp, bearing the disgrace he bore. (Hebrews 11:1-2; 12:1-3, 22-29; 13:13)